# A CONTEMPORARY NORTH AMERICAN PRAYER BOOK

William John Fitzgerald

A CONTEMPORARY NORTH AMERICAN PRAYER BOOK
by William John Fitzgerald

Edited by Marcia Broucek and Gregory F. Augustine Pierce
Cover design by Tom A. Wright
Text design and typesetting by Patricia A. Lynch

The Old Testament texts are taken from the *Inclusive Language Scriptures* published by Priests for Equality. They contain inclusive language throughout. Copyright © 1999, 2000. Used with permission. All rights reserved.

All New Testament quotations are taken from *THE MESSAGE/REMIX: The Bible in Contemporary Language*, edited by Eugene H. Peterson. Copyright © 2003. Used with permission. All rights reserved.

Sources and permissions for other quotations are given on page 155.

Copyright © 2008 by William John Fitzgerald

Published by ACTA Publications, 5559 W. Howard Street, Skokie, IL 60077, 800-397-2282, www.actapublications.com

Library of Cngress number: 2007939185
ISBN: 978-0-87946-335-9
Printed in the United States of America by Versa Press
Year: 15 14 13 12 11 10 09 08
Printing: 15 14 13 12 11 10 9 8 7 6 5 4 3 2 First

# CONTENTS

## PART IV: NORTH AMERICAN LITANIES

Dedicated to the memory
of Brother Bernard Fitzgerald, OCSO,
Guestmaster of New Melleray Abbey (Dubuque, Iowa)
and Our Lady of Assumption (Ava, Missouri),
who lived the Ministry of Hospitality
and the Liturgy of the Hours
into his eighty-first year.

# Introduction

*This prayer book is both "Contemporary" and "North American."*

*It is contemporary because it tries to use current and inclusive language whenever possible, in ways that reflect the usage of people today. The Bible texts come from modern translations or paraphrases, although they are faithful to the meaning and intent of the Scriptures. It also contains some traditional prayers and hymns, sometimes adapted or revised, and many original contemporary pieces. Part I is a simplified version of the Liturgy of the Hours, one of the oldest continuous prayer forms in the history of Christianity. Part II has a new prayer for each of the main seasons of the liturgical year.*

*This book is North American because it uses the places, persons and history of North America as a basis for prayer and meditation. Included in Part III are thirty virtual pilgrimages based on physical locations in Canada, Mexico and the United States. Part IV has two litanies featuring North American saints and sensibilities.*

*William John Fitzgerald*
*Our Lady of Perpetual Help Church*
*Scottsdale, Arizona*

# The Great Story

Fifteen billion years ago—
bursting out of stillness,
billowing forth,
radiating out,
dust gathers,
stars form.

Light
cartwheels,
somersaults,
traces its own trajectory
across the expanding universe.

Eventually—
the forests sing with the wind,
the oceans dance with the moon,
the stars blink their cosmic code.

I was there!
Every element in my body
radiated out with the fireball.

As were all my fellows—
the four-leggeds,
the winged ones,
the finned and the furred.

We all began in radiance
and are meant to live together
in mutually enhancing fellowship.

I was made from radiance.
Made to shine.
Made to burst forth.

This day among fifteen
    billion years
might seem as nothing.
But for me it is everything—
twenty-four hours of potency!

Bless this day,
and all the days of our lives
as they unfurl from your
    gracious hand,
O Creator God!

# Part I

## A North American Liturgy of the Hours

This is an abbreviated and adapted version of the Liturgy of the Hours, which has been used for centuries as a form of contemplative daily prayer. It provides three daily prayer breaks—morning, midday and night. These can be done at any time that is convenient within these wide parameters.

Contemporary versions of three prayers—the Our Father, the Hail Mary, and the Magnificat—are to be said each day as noted. These prayers are positioned first for convenient reference, so you can turn to them when directed (indicated by the names of the prayers in caps). If you prefer to use traditional forms or translations of these prayers, feel free to do so.

Each day of the week has three sets of prayers: Morning (The Hour of Lauds), Midday (The Hour of Nones and the Angelus), and Night (The Hour of Compline). There are certain options offered, which can be chosen either alternately or at random. Each of the midday prayers offers a "North American Island Retreat." You may wish to substitute a different relaxing scene you have experienced, one that has provided you with an "island of peace" moment. You may also use the "Imagine" section of one of the "North American Pilgrimages" in Part III for this meditation.

# Daily Prayers

## The Our Father

Our Father,
your ways and thoughts are far above ours.

May your name be celebrated,
on earth it is in heaven.

May your will be accomplished,
on earth as it is in heaven.

May your reign be realized,
on earth as it is in heaven.

Give us this day
what we need to sustain us.

And forgive us our sins and failings,
as we forgive the sins and failings of others.

Let us not be tempted
to become less than you ask of us.

And keep us from all that would lead us
to be harmed
or to harm others.

For it is your plan,
and your power,
and your glory,
now,
and forever.

Amen.

## The Hail Mary

Hail, Mary.

You are full of grace,
and God is with you.

You are among the happiest of women,
and your child, Jesus, is happy too.

Mary, you are holy,
because you give birth to God.

Pray for us now,
and until the minute we die,
for we are imperfect human beings.

Amen.

## The Magnificat

I'm bursting with God-news;
I'm dancing the song of my Savior God.

God took one good look at me, and look what happened—
I'm the most fortunate woman on earth!

What God has done for me will never be forgotten,
the God whose very name is holy, set apart from all others.

His mercy flows in wave after wave
on those who are in awe before him.

He bared his arm and showed his strength,
scattered the bluffing braggarts.

He knocked tyrants off their high horses,
pulled victims out of the mud.

The starving poor sat down to a banquet;
the callous rich were left out in the cold.

He embraced his chosen child, Israel;
he remembered and piled on the mercies, piled them high.

It's exactly what he promised,
beginning with Abraham and right up to now.

# Sunday Morning Prayer
## The Hour of Lauds

## Opening Prayer

O God, come to my assistance. O God, make haste to help me.
Glory to the One-in-Three as it was in the beginning, is now and
evermore shall be.

## Scripture Reading

Wisdom shines brightly and never fades.
She is seen by those who love Her
and is found by those who seek Her.
She reveals herself
to all who desire to know Her,
and those who rise early to search for Her
will not grow weary of the journey,
for they will find Her seated at the door of their own homes.
To ponder Her is the fullness of Wisdom,
and to be loyal in Her pursuit
is the shortcut to freedom from care.
She searches the far ends of the earth
for those who are worthy of Her,
and She appears to them on their daily path with kindness,
meeting them halfway in all their journeys.

*Wisdom of Solomon 6:12-16*

## Hymn

Come Sophia,
Holy Wisdom, gateway to eternity,
sacred source of all that is,
from long before earth came to be.
In your womb the primal waters
from below and from above
gently rock your sons and daughters
born to wisdom and to love.

Come Sophia,
be a clear compelling presence everywhere.
Still the terror; dry the tears.
Come ease our burdens that we bear.
From the first faint light of morning
through the dark when day is done,
be the mid-wife of our borning,
and the rising of our sun.

*Miriam Therese Winter*

## The Our Father

## Prayer at Rising (Option A)

O God, help me pause in the maelstrom
of my busyness for Sunday rest.
"Shalom!" is your Sunday greeting.
Pour out your spirit of wisdom on me
so I won't grow weary of the journey
and will be refreshed and renewed.
Peace on our house and all who dwell herein.

## Prayer at Rising (Option B)

Praise God! On the seventh day "Sophia," the Feminine Wisdom, guided Mary of Magdala to the empty tomb. When Mary poured out the good news to the disciples, it was like fragrant ointment on their furrowed brows. May we too be anointed with Resurrection gladness.

## Thought for the Day

How we spend our days is, of course, how we spend our lives.

*Annie Dillard*

# Sunday Midday Prayer

## As noon bells ring in our hemisphere, pray:
## The Hours of Nones and Angelus

## Words of Wisdom

The function of spirituality is not to protect us from our times.
The function of spirituality is to enable us to leaven our times,
to stretch our times, to bless our times, to break open our times
to the present will of God.

*Joan Chittister*

## Scripture Beatitude

You're blessed when you're at the end of your rope. With less of
you, there is more of God."

*Matthew 5:3*

## The Hail Mary

## Silence

Relax for a few moments and let go of the morning. Close your
eyes and take several deep breaths until you find your body
relaxing.

## North American Island Retreat

*In your imagination, go to an island of peace. Let yourself be
present on Vancouver Island in British Columbia, Canada.
See in your mind how the fir trees spread a green carpet down
the mountainside to the sea. Look out over the water where a
great white ship is steadily sailing through the strait, under the
bridge and out to sea. Imagine feeling the cool breeze blowing
off the water. Listen for the soft calls of soaring ocean birds.*

*Take a deep breath and smell the tinge of salt in the air. Be there. Be still.*

## BLESSING FOR SUNDAY DINNER

Blessed are you, God of all creation.
Through your generosity we have this bread to eat,
which earth has given and human hands have made.

# Sunday Night Prayer
## The Hour of Compline

### Opening Prayer

O God, come to my assistance. O God, make haste to help me.
Glory to the One-in-Three as it was in the beginning, is now and
evermore shall be.

### Reflection

Tonight, I am thankful for....

### Hymn

Sleep my child and peace be with thee,
all through the night.
Guardian angels God will send thee,
all through the night.
Soft the darkening hours are creeping,
I am faithful; vigil keeping,
all through the night.

While the moon her watch is keeping,
all through the night.
While the worn out world is sleeping,
all through the night.
O'er thy spirit gently hovering,
visions of delight recovering,
breathes a pure and holy feeling,
all through the night.

*Welsh Folk Song (American Adaptation)*

## SCRIPTURE READING

> Trust our God with all your heart,
> and don't rely on your own understanding;
> acknowledge God in everything you do,
> and God will direct your paths.

*Proverbs 3:5*

## THE MAGNIFICAT

## PRAYER FOR THE NIGHT

> I ask forgiveness for....
> I let go of....
> I take to my dreams this affirmation....
> O God, grant me a peaceful night and a perfect end.

# Monday Morning Prayer
## The Hour of Lauds

## Opening Prayer

O God, come to my assistance. O God, make haste to help me.
Glory to the One-in-Three as it was in the beginning, is now and
evermore shall be.

## Scripture Reading

Praise our God from the earth,
you sea creatures and ocean depths,
lightning and hail, snow and mist,
and storm winds that fulfill God's word,
mountains and all hills,
fruit trees and all cedars,
wild animals and all cattle,
small animals and flying birds,
rulers of the earth, leaders of all nations,
all the judges in the world,
young men and young women,
old people and children—
let them praise the Name of our God
whose Name alone is exalted.

*Psalm 148:7-13*

## Hymn

Waning Moon
arcs toward the west,
while Ocean Peaceful
bows toward the sun.

From morning's breaking
till night's footfall,
Mighty Sun
makes its curtain call.

God bless its rising,
God bless its setting,
ever beautiful,
over North America.

## The Our Father

## Prayer at Rising (Option A)

O God, at the beginning of this week,
I align myself with the sun, moon and stars,
with the turning world in motion.
Today my voice will bounce from satellites
back again to earth!
In this era of globalization, may I feel
a kinship with all earthlings.
Bless those who work with me.
Bless my neighbors at home
and my neighbors around the globe.

## Prayer at Rising (Option B)

At the beginning of this new work week, I pray:

God, Creator and giver of all gifts
    bless my time, talent and treasure today
    so that I may be a responsible steward of....

Jesus, apprentice in a family business,
>> bless my efforts today,
>> to make my work world a little better place by....

Mother Mary, eventually a single, sole-supporting mom,
>> bless my work today,
>> which will support....

Saint Joseph, diligent worker, busy at your carpentry,
>> bless my work this week,
>> especially these immediate tasks....

Saint Vincent de Paul, patron of all the poor,
>> bless my thirst for justice
>> especially for the unemployed....

## Thought for the Day

The spirituality of work is a disciplined attempt to align ourselves and our environment with God and to incarnate God's Spirit in the world through all the effort (paid and unpaid) we exert to make the world a better place, a little closer to the way God would have things.

*Gregory Pierce*

# Monday Midday Prayer

## Words of Wisdom

God comes to you disguised as your life.

*Author Unknown*

## Scripture Beatitude

You're blessed when you feel you've lost what is most dear to you.
Only then can you be embraced by the One most dear to you.

*Matthew 5:4*

## The Hail Mary

## Silence

Relax for a few moments and let go of the morning. Close your
eyes and take several deep breaths until you find your body
relaxing.

## North American Island Retreat

*In your imagination, go to an island of peace. Let yourself be
present once again on Vancouver Island in British Columbia. This time, imagine that you are standing in the verdant
Butchart Gardens, surrounded by blooming rose bushes. You
are at the water's edge enjoying the rich fragrance of the roses
and the restful curve of the shoreline. Now look out over the
water: You see whales swimming! As you watch their water
spouts, you smile at their pleasure. Be there. Be still.*

## Lunch Blessing

> Blessed are you, God of all creation.
> Roses bloom from your bounty.
> The food I am about to eat
> comes from the fertile earth.
> Bless the earth!
> Bless the gardens!
> Bless my lunch!

# Monday Night Prayer
## The Hour of Compline

## Opening Prayer

O God, come to my assistance. O God, make haste to help me.
Glory to the One-in-Three as it was in the beginning, is now and
evermore shall be.

## Reflection

Tonight I am thankful for....

## Hymn

The sun has run its course;
this day's journey is complete.
O God, unravel the cares of the day.
Cover me with the stars
and the restful quilt of night.

Comfort my loved ones,
give balm to the sick,
shelter for the homeless,
rest to the bereaved,
and peace through this night.

## Scripture Reading

You created my inmost being
and stitched me together in my mother's womb.
For all these mysteries I thank you—
for the wonder of myself,
for the wonder of your works—
my soul knows it well.

*Psalm 139:13-14*

## The Magnificat

### Prayer for the Night

I ask forgiveness for....
I let go of....
I take to my dreams these affirmations....

O God, grant me a peaceful night and a perfect end.

# Tuesday Morning Prayer
## The Hour of Lauds

## Opening Prayer

O God, come to my assistance. O God, make haste to help me.
Glory to the One-in-Three as it was in the beginning, is now and
evermore shall be.

## Scripture Reading

Let the desert and the wilderness exult!
Let the Arabah rejoice and bloom like the crocus!
Let it blossom profusely,
let it rejoice and sing for joy!
The glory of Lebanon is bestowed on it,
the splendor of Carmel and Sharon.
They will see the glory of Yhwh,
the splendor of our God.
Strengthen all weary hands,
steady all trembling knees.
Say to all those of faint heart:
"Take courage! Do not be afraid!"

*Isaiah 35:1-4*

## Hymn

God is good; say it again.
God is good, without end.
Call for God's love day and night.
To answer this call is God's delight.

Dance with joy; laugh and shout.
It's God's desire, without a doubt.
Live in peace with friend and foe.
Feel God's blessing in your soul.

Angels surround me through the day,
dancing joyfully to guide my way.
Sweet sun, sweet clouds,
all weather is fine.

Give praise to the One,
say thanks to the divine.
Troubles dissolve in God's embrace.
Surrender, surrender to the loving grace.

*David Franzblau*

## The Our Father

## Prayer at Rising (Option A)

"Lebanon, Carmel and Sharon" have lived
  under the shadow of terror,
as do so many places in our world.
O God, deliver me from paralyzing numbness
  to compassionate action;
restore those who live in daily terror to steady courage,
knowing that you "steady all trembling knees."

Praise God! Today my name is not in the morning obituary!
It is a good day.
But I pray for those whose names are there,
and for all who are terrorized or suffer.

## Prayer at Rising (Option B)

God grant me the serenity
to accept the things I cannot change;
courage to change the things I can;
and wisdom to know the difference.

Living one day at a time;
enjoying one moment at a time;
accepting hardships as the pathway to peace.

Taking as God did, this sinful world
as it is, not as I would have it.

Trusting that God will make all things right
if I surrender to God's will,
that I may be reasonably happy in this life
and supremely happy with God
forever in the next.

Amen.

*Attributed to Reinhold Niebuhr*

## Thought for the Day

If you lose hope, somehow you lose the vitality that keeps life
moving, you lose that courage to be, that quality that helps you go
on in spite of it all. And so today, I still have a dream.

*Martin Luther King, Jr.*

# Tuesday Midday Prayer

## As noon bells ring in our hemisphere, pray:
## The Hours of Nones and Angelus

### Words of Wisdom

> Yesterday is history.
> Tomorrow is mystery.
> Today is a gift.
> That is why it is called "the present."

*Eleanor Roosevelt*

### Scripture Beatitude

> You're blessed when you're content
>     with just who you are—no more, no less.
> That's the moment you find yourselves proud owners
>     of everything that can't be bought.

*Matthew 5:5*

### The Hail Mary

### Silence

> Relax for a few moments and let go of the morning. Close your
> eyes and take several deep breaths until you find your body
> relaxing.

## North American Island Retreat

*In your imagination, go to an island of peace. Let yourself be present on Prince Edward Island, nestled in the Gulf of St. Lawrence, Canada. Imagine that you are standing along an empty seaside road, stretching before you to the water's edge. Beside it, sea grass waves in the wind, and just beyond, the ocean laps the shore. See in your mind a white lighthouse on the horizon, set against an azure sky, peeking above a stand of fir trees. The only sound you hear is the rhythmic lap of water onto the waiting sand. A cool summer breeze ruffles the grass along the roadside, and you feel its soft, refreshing caress. Be there. Be still.*

## Lunch Blessing

O God, help me to be content
with who I am and what I have.
Today I have enough to eat;
I am grateful.
Bless the efforts of organizations like Bread for the World,
so that the ill-fed people of our world
might be nourished as I am.
Bless my food and bless their need.

Amen.

# Tuesday Night Prayer
## The Hour of Compline

## Opening Prayer

O God, come to my assistance. O God, make haste to help me.
Glory to the One-in-Three as it was in the beginning, is now and
evermore shall be.

## Reflection

Tonight I am thankful for....

## Hymn

They glisten, sparkle
shape my heart space
like radiant threads
in a star patterned sky.

A constellation of love
formed from my earliest days,
growing in shape and design,
clearer and stronger with age.

Each one supporting me
on the pathway of growth,
each one encouraging me
on the journey of now.

I gaze at my inner sky,
reach toward the pattern,
return the love I receive
and marvel at the beauty.

*Joyce Rupp*

## Scripture Reading

> Friends love you like a sister or brother—
> they are born to give support during adversity.

*Proverbs 17:17*

## The Magnificat

## Prayer for the Night

> I ask forgiveness for....
> I let go of....
> I take to my dreams this affirmation....
>
> O God, grant me a peaceful night and a perfect end.

# Wednesday Morning Prayer
## The Hour of Lauds

## Opening Prayer

O God, come to my assistance. O God, make haste to help me. Glory to the One-in-Three as it was in the beginning, is now and evermore shall be.

## Scripture Reading

Adonai, our God, how majestic is your Name in all the earth!
You have placed your glory above the heavens!
From the lips of infants and children
you bring forth words of power and praise,
to answer your adversaries
and to silence the hostile and vengeful.

When I behold your heavens, the work of your fingers,
the moon and the stars which you have set in place—
what is humanity that you should be mindful of us?
Who are we that you should care for us?
You have made us barely less than God,
and crowned us with glory and honor.
You have made us responsible
for the works of your hands.

Adonai, our God,
how majestic is your Name in all the earth!

*Psalm 8:1-6, 9*

## Hymn

Cell phones, ipods, blogs,
websites, podcasts, networks,
uploading, downloading,
broadcasting, forecasting.

Outsourcing, insourcing,
software, hardware,
instant messaging, email, spam,
Amazon, Ebay,
Google, Yahoo.

Words. Words. Words.
"Rush! Compete! Strive!"
Breaking through the din:
your Words of Life!

To whom can we go?
You speak the words:
"Alpha! Omega!
Kingdom! Salvation!"

Grateful for your connection,
I offer up to you today
my prayer—my GPS—
lofted up above the heavens.

## The Our Father

## Prayer at Rising (Option A)

Good Morning, Americas.
Today's "news" is new,
but old—too much strife
and conflict that stifle life.

Please, God,
let me hear your songs of love.
Let me see your works of beauty.
Let me feel your loving presence.
Let me touch another's heart.

Amen.

*Maureen P. Kane*

## Prayer at Rising (Option B)

May God support us all the day long
till the shadows lengthen,
and the evening comes,
and the busy world is hushed
and the fever of life is over
and our work is done.
Then in his mercy
may he give us a safe lodging
and a holy rest
and peace at last.

*Cardinal John Henry Newman*

## Thought for the Day

There is a pervasive form of contemporary violence…overwork.
The rush and pressure of modern life are a form, perhaps the most
common form, of its innate violence. To allow oneself to be carried
away by a multitude of conflicting concerns, to surrender to too
many demands, to commit oneself to too many projects, to want to
help everyone in everything, is to succumb to violence. The frenzy
of our activism…destroys our inner capacity for peace because it
kills the root of inner wisdom which makes work fruitful.

*Thomas Merton*

# Wednesday Midday Prayer

## As noon bells ring out in our hemisphere, pray: The Hours of Nones and Angelus

## Words of Wisdom

The frog does not drink up the pond in which he lives.

*Native American Proverb*

## Scripture Beatitude

You're blessed when you care. At the moment of being "care-full," you find yourselves cared for.

*Matthew 5:7*

## The Hail Mary

## Silence

Relax for a few moments and let go of the morning. Close your eyes and take several deep breaths until you find your body relaxing.

## North American Island Retreat

*In your imagination, go to an island of peace. Let yourself be present on Mackinac Island in northern Lake Michigan. Imagine that you are sitting on the colonnaded porch of the nineteenth-century Grand Hotel in a white rocking chair, enjoying the expansive vista. Be very aware of the quiet—no motorized vehicles allowed here! The fragrance of lilacs wafts up from the gardens, and you let your slow rocking lull you into a deep calm. Imagine a horse-drawn red carriage approaching, its driver arrayed in crimson livery and black top hat. Its horse clip clops a leisurely pace as it nears the veranda.*

*Be there. Be still. Clip clop. Clip clop. Catch the slow rhythm.*
*Be there. Be still.*

## Lunch Blessing

Tick tock, clip clop.
Tick tock, clip clop.
Tick tock, clip clop.

O God, slow me down.
Calm my stress.
Be near—this food to bless.

# Wednesday Night Prayer
## The Hour of Compline

### Opening Prayer

O God, come to my assistance. O God, make haste to help me. Glory to the One-in-Three as it was in the beginning, is now and evermore shall be.

### Reflection

Tonight I am thankful for....

### Hymn

O gladsome light
of the Father immortal
and of the celestial
sacred and blessed
Jesus our Savior!

Now to the sunset
again thou hast brought us;
and seeing the evening
twilight we bless thee,
praise thee, adore thee!

Father omnipotent!
Son the Life-giver!
Spirit the Comforter!
Worthy at all times
of worship and wonder!

*Henry Wadsworth Longfellow*

## Scripture Reading

I praise our God, who guides me;
even at night my heart teaches me.
I'm always aware of your presence;
you are right by my side, and nothing can shake me.

*Psalm 16:7-8*

## The Magnificat

## Prayer for the Night

I ask forgiveness for....
I let go of....
I take to my dreams these affirmations....

O God, grant me a peaceful night and a perfect end.

# Thursday Morning Prayer
## The Hour of Lauds

### Opening Prayer

O God, come to my assistance. O God, make haste to help me.
Glory to the One-in-Three as it was in the beginning, is now and
evermore shall be.

### Scripture Reading

I sought our God, who answered me
and freed me from all my fears.
Those who look to our God are radiant,
and their faces are never covered with shame.
The poor called out; our God heard
and saved them from all their troubles.
The angel of our God encamps around those
who revere God, and rescues them.
Taste and see how good our God is!
Happiness comes to those who take refuge in our God.

Our God is close to the brokenhearted
and rescues those whose spirits are crushed.

*Psalm 34:4-8, 18*

### Hymn

From the East,
a new dawning,
morning sun to shine upon this house
and dispel the languor of the night.

From the North,
cool refreshment,
to ease the hectic rush of the day,
and bring rest from the bright sun of activity.

From the South,
radiant light to renew
discernment, insight, right thinking,
and all that makes for healing.

From the West,
when the fevered day is done,
completion, a Holy Thursday meal,
and the Peace of Christ to dwell.

## The Our Father

## Prayer at Rising (Option A)

O God, on this Holy Thursday,
let me taste and see your goodness.
Today Jesus fed the twelve.
Today Jesus washed their feet.

I, too, am fed; I am strengthened.
I, too, can serve, wash others' feet.
I join my spirit with every Eucharist:
to give thanks, praise and service.

Let me go forth in love and peace
to serve this hungry world.
May I be bread for hungry hearts,
courage for troubled souls.

## Prayer at Rising (Option B)

> Dorothy Day, tender of the poor,
> may the voices of the homeless
> be heard today.
>
> Cesar Chavez, organizer of the farm workers,
> may the voices of immigrants
> be heard today.
>
> Sacajawea, guide to Lewis and Clark,
> may the voices of the Native Americans
> be heard and listened to today.
>
> Martin Luther King, Jr., martyr for civil rights,
> may the voices of black people
> be heard today.
>
> Susan B. Anthony, fighter for women's rights,
> may the voice of women
> be heard today.
>
> Father Mychal Judge, hero and victim of 9/11,
> may the voice of gay people
> be heard today.

## Thought for the Day

> The saints are the true bearers of light within history, for they are
> men and women of faith, hope and love.
>
> *Pope Benedict XVI*

# Thursday Midday Prayer

## As Angelus Bells ring in our hemisphere, pray:
## The Hours of Nones and Angelus

## Words of Wisdom

> The universe emerges out of an all-nourishing abyss not only fifteen billion years ago but in every moment.... The foundational reality of the universe is this unseen ocean of potentiality.
>
> *Brian Swimme*

## Scripture Beatitude

> You're blessed when you've worked up a good appetite for God. He's food and drink in the best meal you'll ever eat.
>
> *Matthew 5:6*

## The Hail Mary

## Silence

> Relax for a few moments and let go of the morning. Close your eyes and take several deep breaths until you find your body relaxing.

## North American Island Retreat

> *In your imagination, go to an island of peace. Let yourself be present on Martha's Vineyard off the coast of Massachusetts. Imagine that you are sitting on a restaurant deck overlooking the ocean, taking in the tang of saltwater and fresh fish. A small ferry slowly plies its way across the narrow inlet, and you let your breathing slow with it. As you watch fishermen unloading their catch from a trawler, you are reminded of the*

*fish as an ancient eucharistic symbol for Jesus. Imagine Jesus on the dock, blessing the net of fish. Be still. Be there. Speak to Jesus.*

## Lunch Blessing

Brother Jesus, you gave your apostles a net of 153 fish!
In the ocean there is an unseen abundance of sea creatures.
So, too, our universe contains an "unseen ocean of potentiality."

Bless this one day out of the fifteen billion years
    of potency unfolding.
Call up from my hidden resources what is beautiful and lasting.
May this food nourish all the potential of my mind, body
    and spirit.

# Thursday Night Prayer
## The Hour of Compline

### Opening Prayer

O God, come to my assistance. O God, make haste to help me. Glory to the One-in-Three as it was in the beginning, is now and evermore shall be.

### Reflection

Tonight I am thankful for….

### Hymn

O Trinity of blessed light,
O Unity of princely might,
the fiery sun now goes its way;
shed now within our hearts your ray.

To you our morning song of praise,
to you our evening prayer we raise;
O grant us with your saints on high
to praise you through eternity.

To God the Father, heav'nly light,
to Christ revealed in earthly night,
to God the Holy Spirit raise
our equal and unceasing praise.

*Author Unknown (sixth century)*

## Scripture Reading

> Yhwh, you are my God—
> I exalt you! I praise your Name!
> For you do marvelous things,
> planned long ago with steadfast faithfulness.

*Isaiah 25:1*

## The Magnficat

## Prayer for the Night

> I ask forgiveness for....
> I let go of....
> I take to my dreams these affirmations....
>
> O God, grant me a peaceful night and a perfect end.

# Friday Morning Prayer
## The Hour of Lauds

## Opening Prayer

O God, come to my assistance. O God, make haste to help me.
Glory to the One-in-Three as it was in the beginning, is now and
evermore shall be.

## Scripture Reading

My God, my God,
why have you forsaken me?
Why are you so far away,
so far from saving me,
so far from the words of my groaning?

But you, Holy One—
you sit enthroned on the praises of Israel.
Our ancestors put their trust in you,
they trusted and you rescued them;
they cried to you and were saved,
they trusted you and were never disappointed.

But you, Adonai, don't be far off!
My strength, hurry to help me!

Then I will proclaim your Name to my sisters and brothers,
and praise you in the full assembly.

*Psalm 22:1, 3-5, 19, 22*

## Hymn

When the going gets rough,
take it on the chin
with the rest of us,
the way Jesus did.

This is a sure thing:
if we die with him, we'll live with him;
if we stick it out with him, we'll rule with him.

*2 Timothy 2:3, 11*

## The Our Father

## Prayer at Rising (Option A)

O God, help me to bear the daily irritations:
    of busyness and rush,
    of lines and waiting,
    of stresses that stretch my spirit,
    of all the little crosses of inconvenience.

Help me to see the more deeply suffering Christ:
    in the eyes of the sick,
    in the faces of the homeless,
    in the victims of war and violence,
    in the worries and challenges of parenting.

Have mercy especially on these I remember now:
    those who carry burdens hard to bear,
    those whom I love who are far away,
    those with whom I will meet today,
    those upon whom I might have an effect today.

## Prayer at Rising (Option B)

Hear me, four quarters of the world—a relative I am!
Give me the strength to walk on the soft earth,
a relative to all that is.
Give me the eyes to see and the strength to understand,
that I may be like you.
With your power only can I face the winds.

*Black Elk*

## Thought for the Day

(According to Susan Lamb Bean, Navajo people consider the universe
to be in perfect balance except when upset by human misbehavior.
Navajos endeavor to live in *hózhọ'*, which loosely translated means a
state of wholeness and harmony with all that is good and beautiful.)

All is beautiful,
all is beautiful,
all is beautiful indeed.

Now the Mother Earth
and the Father Sky,
meeting, joining one another,
helpmates ever they.

All is beautiful,
all is beautiful,
all is beautiful indeed.

*Inspired by the Navajo*

# Friday Midday Prayer

## Words of Wisdom

Divine wisdom communicates God's view of reality and opens our eyes to the fact that the Kingdom is most accessible in the ordinary routines and difficulties of everyday life and in the most unacceptable (to us) situations.

*Thomas Keating*

## Scripture Beatitude

You're blessed when your commitment to God provokes persecution. The persecution drives you even deeper into God's Kingdom.

Not only that—count yourselves blessed every time people put you down or throw you out or speak lies about you to discredit me. What it means is that the truth is too close for comfort and they are uncomfortable.

*Matthew 5:10-11*

## The Hail Mary

## Silence

Relax for a few moments and let go of the morning. Close your eyes and take several deep breaths until you find your body relaxing.

## North American Island Retreat

*In your imagination, go to an island of peace. Let yourself be present at Liberty Island in New York Harbor and imagine standing below the towering statue of Lady Liberty. Notice the inscription: "Give me your tired, the refuse of your foreign shores…." Offer up whatever sufferings you have endured this week, in union with all who have sacrificed in order to endure in North America—the North American Indians, as well as the immigrants.*

## Lunch Blessing

I bless my food with the sign of the Holy Cross.
So many immigrants came to our shores driven by famine!
Help me not to take my food for granted.
It has come to me through the sweat and toil of the farmer,
and the processing and transportation efforts of so many more.
Praise God for the work.
Praise God for the bounty.

# Friday Night Prayer
## The Hour of Compline

### Opening Prayer

O God, come to my assistance. O God, make haste to help me.
Glory to the One-in-Three as it was in the beginning, is now and
evermore shall be.

### Reflection

Tonight I am thankful for….

### Hymn

Abide with me, fast falls the eventide;
the darkness deepens; Lord, with me abide.
When other helpers fail and comforts flee
help of the helpless, O abide with me.

I need your presence every passing hour;
what but your grace can foil the tempter's power?
Who like yourself my guide and strength can be?
Through cloud and sunshine, Lord, abide with me.

Hold then your cross before my closing eyes;
shine through the gloom and point me to the skies!
Heaven's morning breaks and earth's vain shadows flee;
in life, in death, O Lord, abide with me!

*Henry Francis Lyte*

### Scripture Reading

Like a shepherd you feed your flock,
gathering the lambs and holding them close,
and leading mother ewes with gentleness.

*Second Isaiah 40:11*

## The Magnificat

### Prayer for the Night

I ask forgiveness for….
I let go of….
I take to my dreams these affirmations….

O God, grant me a peaceful night and a perfect end.

# Saturday Morning Prayer
## The Hour of Lauds

## Opening Prayer

O God, come to my assistance. O God, make haste to help me. Glory to the One-in-Three as it was in the beginning, is now and evermore shall be.

## Scripture Reading

If I speak with human eloquence and angelic ecstasy but don't love, I'm nothing but the creaking of a rusty gate. If I speak God's word with power, revealing all his mysteries and making everything plain as day, and if I have faith that says to a mountain, "Jump," and it jumps, but I don't love, I'm nothing. If I give everything I own to the poor and even go to the stake to be burned as a martyr, but I don't love, I've gotten nowhere. So, no matter what I say, what I believe, and what I do, I'm bankrupt without love.

But for right now, until that completeness, we have three things to do to lead us toward that consummation: Trust steadily in God, hope unswervingly, love extravagantly. And the best of the three is love.

*1 Corinthians 13:1-7, 13*

## Hymn

Saturday, first resting day,
Saturday, Mary's day,
Saturday, Earth's day,
Jesus—earthbound.

Buried, a potent seed
in the fertile womb of earth.
Once seeded in Mary
now seeded in clay.

Jesus rests in fertile garden
beneath a black soil quilt.
Rock hewn walls
await the Easter light.

Mary waits in joyful hope
in the shadow of the cross.
Her heart—sword-pierced
but not forsaken.

With the skylark's song
and Magdalene's "Alleluia,"
Mary's heart leaps for joy!
Her soul magnifies the Lord.

## The Our Father

## Prayer at Rising (Option A)

This is the day Mary
let loose of her son
at the holy tomb,
so the wisdom of the ages could be fulfilled.

Unless a grain of wheat
is buried in the ground,
dead to the world,
it is never any more than a grain of wheat.

But if it is buried,
it sprouts
and reproduces itself
many times over.

Bury now my human frailties and sins
so that love can rise out of the shadow of the cross
and the coldness of the tomb,
and bloom in my life like fragrant Easter lilies.

## Prayer at Rising (Option B)

May we be pregnant with hope,
trusting that the reign
of your son will one day dawn
and spill its radiance
even in the darkest corners
of our world.
Teach us to live in unity,
shelter us from despair.
Inspire us to act justly,
to revere all that God has made.
Root us ever more firmly
in the peace of Jesus.

Amen.

*from the Litany of Mary of Nazareth*

## Thought for the Day

I firmly believe that our salvation depends on the poor.

*Dorothy Day*

# Saturday Midday Prayer

## As noon bells ring in our hemisphere, we pray: The Hour of Nones and Angelus

## Words of Wisdom

The Catholic imagination, captivated by grace which it senses lurking everywhere, does not easily give up on the salvation of anyone.

*Andrew Greeley*

## Scripture Beatitudes

You're blessed when you get your inside world—your mind and heart—put right. Then you can see God in the outside world.

You're blessed when you can show people how to cooperate instead of compete or fight. That's when you discover who you really are, and your place in God's family.

*Matthew 5:8-9*

## The Hail Mary

## Silence

Relax for a few moments and let go of the morning. Close your eyes and take several deep breaths until you find your body relaxing.

## North American Island Retreat

*In your imagination, go to an island of peace. Let yourself be present on the Mexican Island of Cozumel. Imagine that you are scuba diving in aquamarine water. As you meander above the coral shelf, you see the many colored fish as they lazily swim by. Feel yourself floating in the water, buoyed by the currents, bathed in the deep water peace. Be there. Be still.*

## Lunch Blessing

O God, today I remember those who seem cut off from the banquet of life:

> my alienated relatives and friends away from the Eucharist,
> the many hard working migrants who face rejection,
> the starving multitudes around the earth.

Help them to find their place in God's family.
Lift up their hearts and lead them to the nourishment they need.
Help them—and me—to discover amazing

> "grace lurking everywhere."

I am grateful for being fed in body and spirit.

# Saturday Night Prayer
## The Hour of Compline

## Opening Prayer

O God, come to our assistance. O God, make haste to help me.
Glory to the One-in-Three as it was in the beginning, is now and
evermore shall be.

## Reflection

Tonight I am thankful for....

## Hymn

Mother dearest, Mother fairest,
help of all who call on thee,
Virgin purest, brightest, rarest,
help us, help, we cry to thee.

Lady help in pain and sorrow,
sooth those racked on beds of pain;
may the golden light of morrow
bring them health and joy again.

Mary, help us, help, we pray.
Mary, help us, help, we pray.
Help us in all care and sorrow,
Mary, help us, help, we pray.

*Traditional Marian Hymn*

## Scripture Reading

Adonai, you are my shepherd—
I want nothing more.
You let me lie down in green meadows,
you lead me beside restful waters,
you refresh my soul.

*Psalm 23:1-3*

## The Magnificat

## Prayer for the Night

I ask forgiveness for....
I let go of....
I take to my dreams this affirmation....

O God, grant me a peaceful night and a perfect end.

# PART II

# NORTH AMERICAN
# SEASONAL PRAYERS

*These are specific prayers for each of the liturgical seasons.
They can be used for private prayer or group prayer.*

# Advent Season

## Waiting in the Dark: The Color Purple

### Waiting for the Son

The waning sun
has gone its way.
Down from Alaska
through Manitoba.

Snow sweeps over
Alberta's fields.
And we long
for sun's return.

Down, down, down,
past Taos and Juarez.
Winter's shadows
cover North America.

We are an Advent people,
waiting for the sun,
and for the Son.
May we live in joyful hope.

In the midst of winter's dark,
open the windows of my soul
so the Christ-light can shine in.
Maranatha! Come, Lord Jesus!

# Christmas Season
## The Feast of Light: The Color Gold

### Tomorrow Shall Be My Dancing Day

Tomorrow shall be my dancing day.
I would my true love did so chance
to see the legend of my play,
to call my true love to the dance.
Sing O my love, O my love, my love, my love;
this I have done for my true love.

In a manger laid and wrapped I was,
so very poor, this was my chance,
betwixt an ox and a silly poor ass,
to call my true love to my dance.
Sing O my love, O my love, my love, my love;
this I have done for my true love.

Then up to heaven I did ascend,
where now I dwell in sure substance
on the right hand of God that mankind
may come into the general dance.
Sing O my love, O my love, my love, my love;
this I have done for my true love.

*Traditional English Carol*

# Ordinary Time

## The Greening and Growing Season:
## The Color Green

### Bless Our Land

Bless our land from sea to sea.
Bless the fields giving life to me.
Bless the earth beneath my feet.
Bless the food we have to eat.

And yet, Creator God,
This is not "ordinary time."

This is extraordinary time,
when fertile earth lies supine,
forests are despoiled,
deserts are cursed by drought,
icebergs are melted by global warming,
bringing chaos out of paradise.

What I do for the earth,
I do for all the children.
Let the earth be for them
no desert, but precious gem.

Bless these children.
Bless their future life.
Bless the earth,
the womb of life.

Bless: (names of children you know)....

# Lenten Season
## Getting Down To Earth: The Color Purple

*Thomas Berry in* Evening Thoughts *reminds us that in the whole universe it is planet earth—with all its wonder—that is the meeting place between the divine and the human.*

*Deborah Halter reminds us in the article "The Riches of Being Downwardly Mobile" that "chronic living beyond our means is really only a way of trying to fill the emptiness in our souls."*

*Patriarch Bartholomew I of Constantinople challenges us that each of us is called to make the crucial distinction between what we want and what we need. Only through such self denial, through our willingness sometimes to forgo and to say "no" or "enough," will we rediscover our true human place in the universe.*

### Lenten Letting Go

> O God,
> day by day in this Lenten season
> help me to accept the little crosses
> of sluggish traffic,
> of waiting in line,
> of recorded responses,
> of folks who rub me the wrong way.
>
> O God,
> help me to make this a time
> to "get down to earth,"
> to simplify my life style,
> to let go of pretenses,
> to retreat from consumerism,
> to fast and abstain—
> a time for rending hearts,
> not garments.

O God,
help me realize I need not search for crosses.
They mark the lives of so many who suffer.
Let me break beyond the boundaries
of my self-concern and narrow vision.
Make this a Lent for others, with others.

# Easter Season

## The Season of Resurrection:
## The Colors White and Gold

"Who will roll back the stone from the tomb for us?" Then they looked up, and saw that it had been rolled back—it was a huge stone—and walked right in.

*Mark 16:3-4*

### Casting Away Stones

O God, let us cast away these stones:
>The heavy stone of fear.
May the risen Christ cast away this stone.
>The heavy stone of injustice.
May the risen Christ cast away this stone.
>The heavy stone of despair.
May the risen Christ cast away this stone.
>The heavy stone of misunderstanding.
May the risen Christ cast away this stone.
>The heavy stone of worry.
May the risen Christ cast away this stone.
>The heavy stone of addiction.
May the risen Christ cast away this stone.
>The heavy stones of all that burdens me.
May the risen Christ cast away these heavy stones.

# Pentecost Season

## The Season of Fire and Wind:
## The Color Crimson

## Seize Us

From depths of tears and chaos,
Holy Spirit, seize us;
raise us from the murky deep—
out of swirling and choking waters.

Emerge from the cyclonic center
of our inner chaos.
Deliver us from the eye of the storm.
Energy of the Spirit, move us.

I pray for myself and these I love
who linger in chaos.
Consoling Spirit, hover near cold tombs.
Fire of the Spirit, warm us.

When we are bogged down,
and tomorrow seems a dark dream,
Spirit Wind, rattle our windows.
Lightning Spirit, waken us.

Stir us from inertia,
fear and cynicism.
Change "Life is not fair!"
to "We can! We will!"

# PART III

# THIRTY NORTH AMERICAN
# PILGRIMAGES

The spiritual reflections in this section are "imaginary" pilgrimages to sacred sites in North America. Even if you have not been to a particular site or cannot physically travel there, I encourage you to go there in your mind and connect with the spiritual energy of each site. As you allow yourself to make these mental pilgrimages to Holy Ground, speak to God about your particular needs and those of others. If you have access to the Internet, you can often download a photo of a site to use as a focal point for your meditation.

These virtual pilgrimages are each meant to provide one prayer experience. You might do one a day for a month, or you can take one anytime you feel the need. The important thing is to give yourself time. Proceed in a slow and contemplative manner. Relax, take your time, linger as long as you can to absorb the spiritual beauty and energy these sites provide. Once you have become familiar with the methodology, you can even compose your own meditations based on other holy places you have visited personally.

# Pilgrimage to the Alamo, San Antonio, Texas

## Opening Prayer

O God, your divine energy fills North America with special places of great beauty and healing consolation. As I make a prayerful, imaginary pilgrimage to this holy ground, I bring to my prayer those in need and place them with me at these natural sources of your spirit. Hear these intentions for which I pray....

## Scripture Reading

That is my parting gift to you: Peace. I don't leave you the way you're used to being left—feeling abandoned, bereft. So don't be upset. Don't be distraught.

*John 14:27*

## Imagine

*"Remember the Alamo!" Yes, remember. Whether you are of Anglo or Latino or Native American or some other descent. Go back to the beginning. Stately cottonwoods with their golden autumn leaves stand as sentinels along the San Antonio River in Texas.*

*Imagine the Native American tribes in the 1500s, gathering there for prayer and for shelter from marauding bands. They knew neither Anglos nor Latinos nor Asians nor Africans nor any other immigrant group.*

*Years later, to the east of the river, Native American and brown-robed padres place yellow stone upon stone to build a house of God, a house of peace. That is when the familiar shape of the Alamo building that we know today first took form.*

*Now, imagine another scene: The Alamo has been expropriated into a fort, and the house of peace has become a house of war. Finally, the firing stops. The Alamo grows silent. Its defenders lie prostrate, its conquerors exhausted.*

*And so the Alamo means many things to many people: heroism, conquest, peaceful refuge.*

*Be still and imagine the many images of the Alamo.*

### CONCLUDING PRAYER

O God, help me remember that North America is made up of many different people, all with their own prayers....

# Pilgrimage to Arlington Cemetery, Arlington, Virginia

## Opening Prayer

O God, your divine energy fills North America with special places of great beauty and healing consolation. As I make a prayerful, imaginary pilgrimage to this holy g round, I bring to my prayer those in need and place them with me at these natural sources of your spirit. Hear these intentions for which I now pray....

## Scripture Reading

But those who wait for Yhwh
find a renewed power:
They soar on eagle's wings.

*Isaiah 40:31*

## Imagine

*In Arlington Cemetery, the gravestones stand row upon row. On any given morning, funeral processions line their way to final resting places. Be there. See a flag-draped caisson lumbering down the path. Its wheels creak. Before it plods a rider-less horse with boots backwards in the stirrups. Notice a hillside of stark beauty—the white shimmering stones against the verdant green grass. Pause and remember the slain warriors of all nations who have been cut down by war. Listen to their call for permanent peace. Hear the poignant sound of Taps.*

*Let Arlington stand for all the burial places in North America: the ice floes of the Northwest Territories, where the dead are loosed into the sea; the dusty burial grounds of Central America, where families gather to remember on "The Day of the Dead"; the cemeteries in every town and every place, for none of us lives forever in our mortal flesh.*

*Now in your imagination go to the burial places that are special to you, where your dearest loved ones lie. Be there. Remember. Be still. Pray:*

*Dear ones,*
*I loved you in your living.*
*I loved you in your suffering.*
*I loved you in your dying.*
*And I love you beyond death—*
*neither confined by time*
*nor stifled by space.*

## Concluding Prayer

God of the Living, let me be lifted up now on eagles' wings as I remember all those who have died....

# Pilgrimage to the Basilica of Saint Anne de Beaupré, Quebec, Canada

## Opening Prayer

O God, your divine energy fills North America with special places of great beauty and healing consolation. As I make a prayerful, imaginary pilgrimage to this holy ground, I bring to my prayer those in need and place them with me at these natural sources of your spirit. Hear these intentions for which I pray....

## Scripture Reading

They had come to hear him and to be healed of their ailments.

*Luke 6:18*

## Imagine

*Beyond Quebec City in Canada, fertile valleys and wooded hillsides roll toward the horizon. And then something magnificent rises up before our eyes—the great, gray, stone towers of the church of Saint Anne du Beaupré. This imposing edifice rises up with nothing tawdry to surround it—only the beauty of the Quebec countryside.*

*This is the sight that so many wounded pilgrims long to see as they flock here from north, south, east and west to seek healing at this holy shrine.*

*Imagine walking up the stone steps and through the great doors. Turn to the left and notice a chapel before you. A haze of incense lingers—the scent print of prayer.*

*As you come closer, you see a startling sight: Rows upon rows of crutches and canes hang on the wall over the altar, left here as an offering of thanks for healings. They are among the many favors obtained at this holy site through the intercession of the mother of Mary, good Saint Anne.*

*There are other miracles that can only be kept in grateful hearts: the lonely imploring Saint Anne for help in finding a friend or a spouse, childless couples asking Saint Anne to be blessed with a child, lost souls looking to Saint Anne to be found again.*

*You are here with the other pilgrims. Now is the time for you to ask for what you need.*

## Concluding Prayer

Good Saint Anne, holding the child Mary on one arm, reach out with the other to accept my pleading....

# Pilgrimage to the Beach
# at Saint Augustine, Florida

## Opening Prayer

O God, your divine energy fills North America with special places of great beauty and healing consolation. As I make a prayerful, imaginary pilgrimage to this holy ground, I bring to my prayer those in need and place them with me at these natural sources of your spirit. Hear these intentions for which I pray....

## Scripture Reading

Walking along the beach of Lake Galilee, Jesus saw two brothers: Simon (later called Peter) and Andrew.

*Matthew 4:18*

## Imagine

*Saint Augustine, for whom this city was named, said that faith is to believe what we do not see, and that the reward of faith is to see what we believe.*

*It is April in the year 1513. Waves lap against the white sands of a pristine beach. Palm trees stretch for miles. A Spanish galleon lies at anchor, its white sails fluttering against an azure sky. Spanish soldiers heavily laden in upper body armor wade through the surf. They are wary. Their helmets flash in the sun. The stillness is broken only by the washing of the waves across the sand.*

*Behind them, a grey-robed Padre lifts up a crucifix and blesses the new land.*

*Natives peer out from dense foliage and are rightly wary of these strangers, for new diseases and flashing swords will come in the shadow of the cross. Eventually a Dominican priest, Bartolomé de las Casas, the "Prophet of the Americas," will defend their humanity against those interested only in gold.*

*Ponce de Leon, seeking the "Fountain of Youth," has ventured upon a magnificent peninsula, which shall be called Florida, or "Land of Flowers." He has left his footprints upon its upper east coast, where eventually the first permanent European settlement in the present United States will be established in 1565.*

*You are there with Ponce de Leon. Sit down on the sandy beach. See the holy cross silhouetted against the sky. Hear the rustle of the palm leaves and the sighing of the wind. Decide for yourself what you seek: gold, the fountain of youth, the dignity of all people.*

## CONCLUDING PRAYER

O God, help me chose wisely from among the many things I seek....

# Pilgrimage to
## Aurora Village, Yellow Knife,
## Northwest Territories, Canada

## Opening Prayer

O God, your divine energy fills North America with special places of great beauty and healing consolation. As I make a prayerful, imaginary pilgrimage to this holy ground, I bring to my prayer those in need and place them with me at these natural sources of your spirit. Hear these intentions for which I pray....

## Scripture Reading

The Life light was the real thing:
Every person entering Life
he brings into Light.

*John 1:9*

## Imagine

*It is a late autumn night and a native guide from the "Only Aboriginal Tourism Guide Company in the World" hitches your dog sled, and you climb aboard. You are warm enough in your furry parka. The sled jerks and you are off, soon gliding over the crisp snow.*

*Only the occasional yelps of the dogs puncture the brooding silence of the night. Eventually you arrive at a frozen lake framed by towering trees. The dogs pull up. The pure, cold air wafts only the strong scent of the surrounding pines. And now you can see more than the wagging tails of the Huskies. Look up now above the trees and toward the horizon. There the Divine Artist paints the sky with the Northern Lights.*

*The ultimate Creator of all beauty splashes purples, greens and pinks across the vault. The incandescent colors swirl and dance across the sky. And, at the edge of the multicolored horizon, brilliant stars dazzle, blink, nod. Remain in silent communion with the universe.*

*Now, ponder this mystery: Sometimes, when we find ourselves distraught and shivering in a cold and dark wilderness at our darkest moment, we may be closest to the light.*

## Concluding Prayer

O Great Spirit of the Northern Lights, brighten my view and warm my spirit on these dark things about which I pray....

# Pilgrimage to the Beach at Santa Barbara, California

## Opening Prayer

O God, your divine energy fills North America with special places of great beauty and healing consolation. As I make a prayerful, imaginary pilgrimage to this holy ground, I bring to my prayer those in need and place them with me at these natural sources of your spirit. Hear these intentions for which I pray....

## Scripture Reading

God called the dry ground "Earth" and the gathering of the waters "Sea." And God saw that this was good.

*Genesis 1:10*

## Imagine

*You are seated on a veranda high in the hills of Santa Barbara, California.*

*Beneath you are the red tiled roofs of white washed houses. Bougainvilleas of red and purple spill over the fences that divide the houses. And way below, the blue Pacific with its rippled white caps rolls in upon the shore.*

*Watch the tide as it rhythmically breaks upon the shore.*

*It breaks and goes out again.*

*Breaks and goes out again.*

*Breaks and goes out again.*

*Hear the water faintly swishing on the sand. Stay with the rhythms of the waves until you are perfectly relaxed.*

*Now hear the faint ringing of bells from the tower of the old Santa Barbara Mission.*

*Savor the sound. Bless the earth and the sea.*

## CONCLUDING PRAYER

Saint Barbara, heroic woman of old Italy, help me see the beauty of North America and accept my role in preserving it....

# Pilgrimage to the
# Black Elk / John Neihardt Park,
# Blair, Nebraska

## Opening Prayer

O God, your divine energy fills North America with special
places of great beauty and healing consolation. As I make a
prayerful, imaginary pilgrimage to this holy ground, I bring to
my prayer those in need and place them with me at these natural
sources of your spirit. Hear these intentions for which I pray....

## Scripture Reading

As they led him off, they made Simon, a man from Cyrene who
happened to be coming in from the countryside, carry the cross
behind Jesus.

*Luke 23:26*

## Imagine

*In Nebraska, bluffs meander along the edge of the Missouri
River Valley. Close to where Lewis and Clark camped is a
lovely little park where a great mosaic cross rises—the Tower
of Four Winds—the memorial to Black Elk, the Lakota Sioux
Indian holy man, and to John Neihardt, Nebraska's poet
laureate, who made the holy man immortal in his book* Black
Elk Speaks. *Black Elk related to Neihardt how, in his great vision, he saw many hoops making but one circle, with one great
flowering tree to shelter all the children of one mother and one
father. All he saw, Black Elk said, was holy.*

*Wend a pilgrim's way into the park. The wind is always rest-
less on the plains. Just beyond the wire park fence, to your
right, the wind sifts and weaves the fields of golden grain.*

*They bow, as though in prayer. Now look up. At the top of the bluff a cross soars into the blue sky—the Tower of the Winds. Pause to take in the view; the red colors of its tiled surface stand out. Continue your slow ascent. Now you can see that the cross has circular rings emanating from its core and other colored tiles of brown and gold and green.*

*Now look closer still. Notice there is a universal Messiah figure in the center with arms stretched out in blessing. But it also resembles the trunh of a tree of life—centered in a circle of light, ever widening until it reaches the outer circle, the brilliant blue of the sky. Around the rim of the outer circle, cottonwood leaves are seen with birds gathering to sing in the tree of life. The cross arms of the design represent the crossing of the roads—the horizontal black road of difficulties that we all must walk and the vertical good red road of life that leads from the Great Spirit to Mother Earth. Notice black-hooded human figures on the horizontal bars making their way to the center.*

*Meditate on your place on the two roads.*

CONCLUDING PRAYER

Great Spirit, may those in need be nourished by the tree of life and strengthened by the circle of love, especially....

# Pilgrimage to
## *El Santuario de Chimayó,*
## Chimayó, New Mexico

## Opening Prayer

O God, your divine energy fills North America with special
places of great beauty and healing consolation. As I make a
prayerful, imaginary pilgrimage to this holy ground, I bring to
my prayer those in need and place them with me at these natural
sources of your spirit. Hear these intentions for which I pray....

## Scripture Reading

He said this and then spit in the dust, made a clay paste with the
saliva, rubbed the paste on the blind man's eyes, and said, "Go
wash in the Pool of Siloam."

*John 9:6-7*

## Imagine

*Situated among the rolling brown hills and green piñon trees
of rural New Mexico stands the renowned "healing sanctuary"
of Chimayó. You enter an outer courtyard by passing through
an arched entryway that frames the church's brown adobe façade. A sun-splashed walkway leads from there to the church's
main door. The church's double towers soar skyward.*

*Upon entering the church, your vision is filled with the sanctu-
ary scene. The altar screen is of delicately carved yellow wood
with ten painted panels which frame its central figure, the
"miraculous crucifix." The Christ figure's head leans upon his
right shoulder in utter agony. Stop and meditate on the image.
Speak to the*

*suffering Christ for those who suffer and for whom you pray on this pilgrimage.*

*Enter one of its side chapels. It is a riot of colors. Every variety of icon and statue stands on shelves giving testimonies of gratitude for favors received. Notice a pair of baby shoes near the image of Santo Niño de Atocha that symbolize the belief that the Christ Child wears out his shoes during the night walking about doing good.*

*Now enter another side chapel, which possesses the "holy dirt." In the center of this small chapel is a hole in the floor with the dirt below visible. Here at the santuario, pious pilgrims scoop up the blessed dirt to take home or even to ingest. Meditate on the holy dirt: We are smeared with it on Ash Wednesday and reminded that it is our origin. Once Jesus used mud to heal. At the ninth station of the cross, he fell upon the dirt and smeared it with his blood. Stoop and take a handful; let the reddish dirt sift through your fingers. You are grounded!*

## CONCLUDING PRAYER

O Christ, subject both to the earth's travails as well as to its healing, I make these earthly intentions....

# Pilgrimage to the Church of San Francisco de Asís, Rancho de Taos, New Mexico

## Opening Prayer

O God, your divine energy fills North America with special places of great beauty and healing consolation. As I make a prayerful, imaginary pilgrimage to this holy ground, I bring to my prayer those in need and place them with me at these natural sources of your spirit. Hear these intentions for which I pray....

## Scripture Reading

Jesus entered, stood among them, and said, "Peace be to you."

*John 20:19-20*

## Imagine

*No wonder the parish church of Saint Francis of Assisi in Taos, New Mexico, draws a myriad of artists and artisans to its doors. It is seen by many as the crown jewel of adobe churches in the Southwest. Its image has been made familiar by paintings and photographs by artists such as Georgia O'Keeffe and Ansel Adams.*

*Imagine standing in an archway at the entrance to a garden, with a long flagstone walkway proceeding ahead of you to the church entrance. Every reproduction of this scene seems to be three dimensional. A white cross stands right in front of the main door, casting its shadow back against the church. The church is the brown adobe of the desert. It is flanked on each side by two bell towers surmounted by white crosses. The central façade has a round cupola crowned with another white cross. The overall effect is a calm that invites contemplative pause.*

*There is something very special about the lighting in New Mexico. In the brightness of day the adobe is a calming brown. When the sun sets or rises, the church takes on the color of soothing amber.*

*Imagine yourself looking through the archway at sunset. Hear the soft pealing of the bells. Breathe in and out slowly. Find your body relaxing. Sit on a campstool and watch the moon peeking over the edge of the church roof as the shadows of the large cross lengthen down the walkway. Be still. Be at peace.*

## Concluding Prayer

Good Saint Francis, make me an instrument of your peace in the following ways....

# Pilgrimage to the Golden Gate Bridge, San Francisco

## Opening Prayer

O God, your divine energy fills North America with special places of great beauty and healing consolation. As I make a prayerful, imaginary pilgrimage to this holy ground, I bring to my prayer those in need and place them with me at these natural sources of your spirit. Hear these intentions for which I pray....

## Scripture Reading

Fling wide the gates,
open the ancient doors,
and the Glorious Liberator will come in!

*Psalm 24:7*

## Imagine

*You are standing at the foot of the great Golden Gate Bridge at the entrance of the San Francisco Harbor. Look up through the orange beams. Far above—an unfamiliar noise. It is the hum of traffic as it moves over the grated floor of the big bridge.*

*Look now and see a ship passing under the bridge. The ocean water laps against the shore.*

*Far across the bay on the opposite shore loom the golden California hills.*

*Men and women have sailed under this bridge on their way to adventure and war. And men and women have returned home again, a little wiser, passing beneath its welcoming girders.*

*This is the "Golden Gate" to the wide Pacific Ocean and to the beautiful "city by the bay." Long before the bridge was here, Father Junipero Serra, the founder of the California missions, stood where you stand and dedicated this harbor to St. Francis of Assisi.*

*Recall to mind the song made famous by Tony Bennett: "I Left My Heart in San Francisco."*

## CONCLUDING PRAYER

Saint Francis of Assisi, help open the gate of my heart to the needs of others....

# Pilgrimage to the Basilica of Our Lady of Guadalupe, Mexico City

## Opening Prayer

O God, your divine energy fills North America with special places of great beauty and healing consolation. As I make a prayerful, imaginary pilgrimage to this holy ground, I bring to my prayer those in need and place them with me at these natural sources of your spirit. Hear these intentions for which I pray….

## Scripture Reading

I'm bursting with good news; I'm dancing the song of my Savior God.

*Luke 1:46*

## Imagine

*Now it is called Mexico City. Then—in 1531 on December 9, when Saint Juan Diego saw the Virgin—it was called "Tepeyac." In his book,* Guadalupe: A Mother for the New Creation, *Virgil Elizondo declares Mount Tepeyac to be the mountain of the Transfiguration of the Americas. For here, in the conversation between Our Lady and Juan Diego, a blessing is proclaimed for the poor, the meek, the lowly, the sorrowing, the peacemakers and the persecuted of the New World. Today, a great church rises up here in honor of Our Lady.*

*But now go back in imagination to that primal moment when Juan Diego, just an ordinary fellow—an Indian peasant— considered lowly by the Spanish conquistadors, was trudging along, only to be stunned by a blazing radiance. There, before him on the hill of Tepeyac, in the scrabble of mesquite and weeds, a beautiful, dark skinned, young and pregnant girl appears and speaks. All the colors of her raiment are radiant and vivid—her green coat is covered with gold stars, and beneath the coat she wears a lovely pink dress. And all about her, the earth glows. Sun-like rays dance from her shoulders.*

*Feel the December chill. Now look what is spreading out onto Juan's ragged cloak laid upon the ground: Red roses! In the wintertime! Pick one up. Touch its fragile bloom. Smell the rose fragrance as more drop from the beautiful girl's hand.*

*She speaks to him and honors him as no peasant had been honored before. She smiles at him and says "Man of dignity—Juan Diego!" And she smiles at you as well.*

## Concluding Prayer

Finish this pilgrimage with this simple peasant's prayer: "*Madre Mia!* You cannot say you can't. And you won't say you won't. So you will. Won't you?"

# Pilgrimage to the Chapel of the Holy Cross, Sedona, Arizona

## Opening Prayer

O God, your divine energy fills North America with special places of great beauty and healing consolation. As I make a prayerful, imaginary pilgrimage to this holy ground, I bring to my prayer those in need and place them with me at these natural sources of your spirit. Hear these intentions for which I pray....

## Scripture Reading

Don't run from suffering; embrace it. Follow me and I'll show you how. Self help is no help at all. Self sacrifice is the way, my way, to finding yourself, your true self.

*Matthew 16:25-26*

## Imagine

*Sedona, Arizona, is at the edge. Some say it is the vortex of unique earth energies. Below spreads the Valley of the Sun—and the cactus-filled Sonoran desert. Above it rises Oak Creek Canyon, edged by evergreens. Oak Creek surges and splashes down its channel. Surrounding Sedona are brilliant red canyon walls.*

*Perched high on these scarlet parapets is the Chapel of the Holy Cross. After driving up a winding road, you leave your car at the entrance to the chapel. The view from the entrance is stunning. Everywhere you look to south, west and north, red canyon walls soar up into blue skies sprinkled with puffy white clouds.*

*From the doorway of the chapel, soft Gregorian chant echoes against the canyon walls: "Miserere mei Deus…." At the door, a small fountain bubbles. Surrounding it a circle of wild flowers bends in the gentle breeze and scents the air.*

*How fitting that the Holy Cross Chapel would be surrounded on every side by blood red stone. The words of the poet Joseph Mary Plunkett are appropriate here: The thunder and the singing of the birds / Are but his voice / And carven by his power / Rocks are his written words.*

*Let the red rocks speak to you of blood shed, of sufferings borne, of the Holy Cross.*

## CONCLUDING PRAYER

O Christ, at this shrine of your Holy Cross, I place these burdens and seek your healing help….

# Pilgrimage to the Shrine of the Immaculate Conception, Washington, D.C.

## Opening Prayer

O God, your divine energy fills North America with special places of great beauty and healing consolation. As I make a prayerful, imaginary pilgrimage to this holy ground, I bring to my prayer those in need and place them with me at these natural sources of your spirit. Hear these intentions for which I pray....

## Scripture Reading

Jesus took Peter and the brothers James and John, and led them up a high mountain. His appearance changed from the inside out, right before their eyes.

*Matthew 17:2-3*

## Imagine

*Its tower stands tall to the left. In the center an arched façade contains a great circular rose window. Its majestic dome of gold and blue tiles hovers over the horizon, like a religious neighbor to the secular U.S. Capitol dome.*

*Imagine going up the steps and into the interior of the National Shrine of the Immaculate Conception in Washington, D.C. Turn back and look over your shoulder. Displayed above is the great filigreed rose window. Filtered light streams through its colored windows, splashing the floor beneath your feet. Like those at Chartres and Notre Dame, the church's circular shape honors the earth in which the incarnation is rooted and the womb of Mary, whom Catholics believe was conceived without sin.*

*Just as the tower outside points to the transcendent God "beyond," so too the circular window adds the feminine and proclaims the divine as immanent—in our midst—made flesh in the womb of Mary and the birth of Jesus. This is why it is necessary and appropriate to have a national shrine to Our Lady in the midst of the political center of the world.*

## CONCLUDING PRAYER

Our Lady of the Immaculate Conception, remind me always that God has become flesh and lived among us, even when it is hard for me to see it in the midst of my worries and concerns....

# Pilgrimage to the Mission of San José de Laguna, Laguna, New Mexico

## Opening Prayer

O God, your divine energy fills North America with special places of great beauty and healing consolation. As I make a prayerful, imaginary pilgrimage to this holy ground, I bring to my prayer those in need and place them with me at these natural sources of your spirit. Hear these intentions for which I pray....

## Scripture Reading

He said, "Master, I want to see again!" Jesus said, "Go ahead—see again. Your faith has saved and healed you."

*Luke 18:41-42*

## Imagine

*Here in this remote locality in what is now New Mexico, the community of Catholic Christians—the church gathered— prayed and dreamed of a church building in the year 1699. They succeeded, and it remains today.*

*As you approach that lovely church of their dreams, from the outside you are struck by its exterior simplicity. There is one sparkling white tower off center. The façade narrows upward with three serrated edges. Toward the top are two niches with bells. The ancient wooden doors in the center below are carved with the Franciscan coat of arms and the coat of arms of the Bishop of Durango, Mexico, who was the bishop when the church was built.*

*Now open the door; enter and be struck by the explosion of color. The ornate altarpiece of reds and golds and greens reveals the cosmos: the stars and firmament above, with the Holy Trinity. Below are three figures: Saint Barbara, patroness against lightning, firearms, and sudden death, on the right; St. Joseph, the father of Jesus, in the center; Saint John of Nepomuk, the national saint of Bohemia, on the left.*

*Hanging from the ceiling as a canopy over the altar is an animal hide decorated with symbols from the Native American tradition. There are also two striking icons in the church. One is painted on elk hide by the early Franciscans and shows the image of Saint Joseph with carpenter's tools and his hand outstretched to the young boy Jesus. The other prominent shrine also has a young woman draped by an ornate Native American blanket and wearing a headdress of beads and feather. She is "Little Owl"—Blessed Kateri Tekakwitha— the Lily of the Mohawks. Kateri was young, in her twenties when she died, and had eye problems. Imagine Blessed Kateri smiling at you with perfectly healthy eyes.*

## Concluding Prayer

Saint Joseph and Blessed Kateri, allow me to see Jesus in the following people in my life….

# Pilgrimage to
# Saint Jude's Children's Hospital,
# Memphis, Tennessee

## Opening Prayer

O God, your divine energy fills North America with special places of great beauty and healing consolation. As I make a prayerful, imaginary pilgrimage to this holy ground, I bring to my prayer those in need and place them with me at these natural sources of your spirit. Hear these intentions for which I pray....

## Scripture Reading

For an answer Jesus called over a child, whom he stood in the middle of the room, and said, "I'm telling you, once and for all, that unless you return to square one and start over like children, you're not even going to get a look at the kingdom, let alone get in."

*Matthew 18:2-4*

## Imagine

*This is the house of healing founded by the vision of a man who gave away laughter and compassion—Danny Thomas. Let it stand for all the hospitals and care centers of the Americas where the sick are tended and mercy is bestowed.*

*As you approach its entrance, a pair of red wagons is parked at the door. Nearby is a lovely sculpture of children dancing, hand in hand. Ahead of you are parents with children in hand.*

*Enter the front door. Notice some children with shaved heads—crowns of thorns from cancer treatments. Above is a mural of children playing in four different scenes—winter, spring, summer and fall. It is titled "Seasons of Miracles."*

*Take it in.*

*From somewhere down the hall comes the sound of children's laughter. Danny Thomas would be pleased to hear it, for it lifts for a moment the pall of suffering and grief.*

*Saint Jude is the patron saint of miracle prayers answered. This is his house and these are his friends who seek his help.*

*Do not hesitate here to ask for a miracle, while in the end you pray, "Thy will be done."*

## Concluding Prayer

Good Saint Jude, patron of impossible causes, I bring my most difficult petitions to you....

# Pilgrimage to a Hill in Labrador, Canada

## Opening Prayer

O God, your divine energy fills North America with special places of great beauty and healing consolation. As I make a prayerful, imaginary pilgrimage to this holy ground, I bring to my prayer those in need and place them with me at these natural sources of your spirit. Hear these intentions for which I pray....

## Scripture Reading

Adonai is my fortress;
my God is my rock of refuge.

*Psalm 94:22*

## Imagine

*Tonight, in the moonlight, the contrails of trans-Atlantic jets trace across the north sky. Eons earlier, this starry sky guided intrepid sailors on their way to a "new-found land." Leif Erickson and the Vikings were here—and before that? Some say Brendan the Navigator and his Celtic monks. Perhaps they were the first to sing "Ave Maria" on North American shores.*

*This may have been the scene back then: On a rocky and most remote Labrador hill, hooded Irish monks place stone upon stone. They need no mortar. Their tiny cells are corbel style, just as they used in far away Galway.*

*As the early darkness of the north descends upon them, they gather in one stone hut larger than the rest. There they chant the prayer as ancient as the harps of David, the Psalms.*

*Be there with them. Imagine them bowed in a circle. In the center is a lectern holding a calf-skin scripture. Beside it a large candle flickers and glows.*

*Their hooded figures cast shifting shadows on the stone walls. It is time for night prayer, which concludes, then as now, with the hymn, "Salve Regina": Hail, Holy Queen, mother of mercy! Our life, our sweetness, and our hope!*

*Then they retire for the night.*

*When the first streaks of dawn creep upon the ocean rim, they rise again. Their prayer is perhaps Patrick's prayer: "I arise today, through the strength of heaven…."*

## Concluding Prayer

Mother of Mercy, please grant me your help in obtaining the following petitions….

# Pilgrimage to Lake Louise, Banff National Park, Alberta, Canada

✠

## Opening Prayer

O God, your divine energy fills North America with special places of great beauty and healing consolation. As I make a prayerful, imaginary pilgrimage to this holy ground, I bring to my prayer those in need and place them with me at these natural sources of your spirit. Hear these intentions for which I pray....

## Scripture Reading

He climbed into the boat that was Simon's and asked him to put out a little from the shore.

*Luke 5:3*

## Imagine

*The ragged jutting cliffs of the Canadian Rockies hurl up a sentinel's palisade around the blue waters of Lake Louise in Banff National Park in Alberta, Canada. The water is so clear, so clean, so cold.*

*Feel the gentle mountain breeze that ripples the surface of the lake water like a mother gently flouncing the blue blanket of her sleeping child.*

*Sit like a child at the edge of the lake, and let it calm every fear, every anxiety. Enjoy the silence and let it bring restoration to your restless spirit.*

*Think of how much time Jesus spent healing at the edge of holy waters: the pool at Bethsaida, the Sea of Galilee, the*

*Jordan River. Imagine you get into a canoe with Jesus and let him take you out on the lake. Ask him to calm any turbulent waters in your life.*

*Perhaps he will even ask you to walk across the water with him.*

## Concluding Prayer

O God, here at the edge of this holy water, I pray for peace, in my life and in the world....

# Pilgrimage to the Lights
## of Los Angeles

### Opening Prayer

O God, your divine energy fills North America with special places of great beauty and healing consolation. As I make a prayerful, imaginary pilgrimage to this holy ground, I bring to my prayer those in need and place them with me at these natural sources of your spirit. Hear these intentions for which I pray....

### Scripture Reading

The life-light blazed out of the darkness; the darkness couldn't put it out.

*John 1:5*

### Imagine

*It is nighttime in the City of the Holy Angels. The fires of the California coast have gone out for now, but they will return. It is the nature of nature.*

*Tonight, however, you stand on a promontory high up in the hills looking over the flickering lights of the great city. A magic carpet of lights is sprinkled like sparkly stardust out into the very edges of the night. The amber lights flicker and glow. Each light illumines a corner. Each light stands for someone's home, or someone's story. Down below, busy humans watch television, sleep, dream, make love, pray. Some of them work all night.*

*Los Angeles is a city of dreams—starlets hoping to be discovered; actors waiting tables until their first big break; students studying at UCLA, USC, LMU and other great colleges; immigrants and minorities looking for a break.*

*And above them all, "angels of God, our Guardians dear, to whom God's love commits us here" are watching over saint and sinner alike.*

## CONCLUDING PRAYER

O Holy Angels, help me stay sober and awake, for the enemy sometimes goes about in the dark, seeking those for whom I pray....

# Pilgrimage to Notre Dame du Cap-de-la-Madeleine, Trois-Rivières, Quebec

## Opening Prayer

O God, your divine energy fills North America with special places of great beauty and healing consolation. As I make a prayerful, imaginary pilgrimage to this holy ground, I bring to my prayer those in need and place them with me at these natural sources of your spirit. Hear these intentions for which I pray....

## Scripture Reading

She wrapped him in a blanket and laid him in a manger, because there was no room in the hostel.

*Luke 2:7*

## Imagine

*With its ancient roots going back to the first settlers in 1634, the first Marian shrine in Canada, east of Montreal and near Trois-Rivières, has come to be known as "Our Lady of the Cape." From the poorest and humblest of pilgrims to the feet of Pope John Paul II, millions have left their footprints here. Its stone chapel built in 1720 is the oldest church in Canada.*

*Go in imagination to the lovely grounds. There you find the small shrine, and standing behind it, the magnificent new basilica. Walk further and discover a lovely small pond with a small island and a statue of Mary surrounded by greenery.*

*There is a walk around the pond titled "The Rosary Spring." Notice people quietly walking around the water saying the rosary. Today there are some Native Americans in traditional dress. They come from the Northwest Territories—like the Magi of old—to offer homage to Our Lady and her son.*

*Imagine yourself standing at the pond's edge, completely immersed in a circle of prayer. Breathe in the fresh smell of the shrubs and greenery. Think about the people who have come before you...and those who will follow you.*

## Concluding Prayer

Our Lady of the Cape, please hear my prayer for my intentions and those of all pilgrims....

# Pilgrimage to the Cathedral of Mary, Our Queen, Baltimore, Maryland

## Opening Prayer

O God, your divine energy fills North America with special places of great beauty and healing consolation. As I make a prayerful, imaginary pilgrimage to this holy ground, I bring to my prayer those in need and place them with me at these natural sources of your spirit. Hear these intentions for which I pray....

## Scripture Reading

Jesus' mother told him, "They're just about out of wine." Jesus said, "Is that any of our business, Mother—yours or mine? This isn't my time. Don't push me." She went ahead anyway, telling the servants, "Fill the pots with water."

*John 2:2-5*

## Imagine

*This beautiful cathedral is relatively new, but it is built over the footprints of the first Catholic settlers seeking their own place in what is now the United States. They arrived in 1634 seeking religious freedom, and they named the beautiful countryside "Mary's Land." Each March 25th, which is the feast of Our Lady's Annunciation, is also "Maryland Day."*

*Enter the Cathedral and pause before Mary's shrine. Our Lady's gold statue is framed by a golden rectangle with rays emanating all around her and three sets of golden rays extending beyond the frame. She stands upon a globe, and at her feet on each side two horizontal golden angels support the base upon which she stands.*

*This church is dedicated to Mary, Our Queen. Sometimes this is hard for us to relate to, since we are so committed to democracy in North America. However, Mary is a queen in a much different way than most royalty. First, she is of peasant stock herself, and so she can relate to the poor and suffering. Second, she is the Mother of Sorrows, and so she can relate to our grief and sorrow. Third, she is a servant queen, seeking only to intercede with her son so the wedding feast can continue.*

*Imagine Mary as your mother, encouraging you to do something you are not prepared to do.*

## Concluding Prayer

Holy Queen, Mother of Mercy, our advocate, turn your eyes of mercy toward me as I pray for these concerns....

# Pilgrimage to
# the Mission Bell of Maryknoll,
# Ossining, New York

## Opening Prayer

O God, your divine energy fills North America with special places of great beauty and healing consolation. As I make a prayerful, imaginary pilgrimage to this holy ground, I bring to my prayer those in need and place them with me at these natural sources of your spirit. Hear these intentions for which I pray....

## Scripture Reading

A sight to take your breath away!
Grand processions of people
telling all the good things of God!

*Romans 10:16*

## Imagine

*At most pilgrimage sites, the visual effects are what are most stunning. At Maryknoll, in Ossining, New York, the most lasting memory may be a pealing sound that echoes through the years. It summons attention and seizes the imagination. It is the sound of a bell tolling out a mission.*

*Maryknoll is the headquarters of the USA's own missionary society. Today is "Mission Sending Day," and from the center of this campus a bell rings out loud and clear. This is the mission bell that has sent Maryknoll missionaries far and wide throughout the world. Through the years, countless Maryknollers—priests, sisters, brothers and lay volunteers—have gone forth "to tell all the good things of God."*

*It sent Bishop Francis X. Ford and others to China and eventual death at the hand of the Chinese Communists. It sent the Maryknoll team of Sisters Maura Clark and Ita Ford and lay volunteer Jean Donovan from the Archdiocese of Cleveland to El Salvador to be murdered by death squads. It has sent missionaries to Africa, Japan, the Philippines and many other countries since 1911.*

*Many Catholics and other Christians in the United States have responded to the worldwide cry of the poor because of the mission bell at Maryknoll. Listen to it ring once again.*

## CONCLUDING PRAYER

Mother Mary, let me hear from the mission bell at your namesake Maryknoll the cry of all those who are suffering from injustice....

# Pilgrimage to Niagara Falls, Ontario and New York

## Opening Prayer

O God, your divine energy fills North America with special places of great beauty and healing consolation. As I make a prayerful, imaginary pilgrimage to this holy ground, I bring to my prayer those in need and place them with me at these natural sources of your spirit. Hear these intentions for which I pray....

## Scripture Reading

The water I give will be an artesian spring within, gushing fountains of endless life.

*John 4:14*

## Imagine

*Perhaps letting go, letting be, and letting God is the lesson offered to us by the mighty Niagara Falls. So much power and energy, and yet it is only as it lets go and plunges 193 feet into the chasm that its magnificent beauty is born in thunder and mist.*

*Stand beside it. Look down into the turbulence below. See the rainbow hovering in the mists.*

*Look beside you. A newly-married couple holds hands and stands transfixed. Their love will need to learn the waters' lesson of letting go, over and over.*

*Feel the platform on which you stand tremble. Every second 212,000 cubic feet of water hurtle down and splash on the rocks below.*

*Be there. Listen. Feel the energy vibrate in the vessels of your own body.*

*Let the soft spray caress your face.*

## Concluding Prayer

Here, in this site of massive energy whose power blesses both Canada and the USA, I pray for new energy to....

# Pilgrimage to the University of Notre Dame, South Bend, Indiana

## Opening Prayer

O God, your divine energy fills North America with special places of great beauty and healing consolation. As I make a prayerful, imaginary pilgrimage to this holy ground, I bring to my prayer those in need and place them with me at these natural sources of your spirit. Hear these intentions for which I pray....

## Scripture Reading

Jesus saw his mother and the disciple he loved standing near her. He said to his mother, "Woman, here is your son." Then to the disciple, "Here is your mother." From that moment the disciple accepted her as his own mother.

*John 19:26-27*

## Imagine

*It is a lovely October Saturday at the University of Notre Dame in South Bend, Indiana. Across the golden leafed campus, throngs converge on the yellow-bricked football stadium. Stand facing the other way and look up at Our Lady, standing upon the golden dome. There she is, arrayed in gold, bright as the sun.*

*Now move away from the crowds. Take a leisurely walk down from the administration building and arrive at the campus shrine of Our Lady of Lourdes. Before its flickering vigil lights, students and visitors kneel in silent prayer. Mary's statue, as she appeared to Saint Bernadette, stands high up in the grotto. She is clothed in white with a blue sash.*

*Listen carefully now as from the stadium filters the sounds of the marching band and the student body singing with gusto: "Cheer, cheer for old Notre Dame, wake up the echoes cheering her name…."*

*"Old Notre Dame" is not just a university. She is the Lady on the golden dome, the mother of "Touchdown Jesus." Perhaps Mary does not deliver football victories to the University of Notre Dame, but she does watch over the spiritual welfare of all her children there.*

*Imagine that Mary is your mother and that you have taken her into your own home.*

## CONCLUDING PRAYER

Notre Dame, Our Lady, please watch over me, as any mother would, in my times of trouble….

# Pilgrimage to the Basilica of Nuestra Señora de San Juan de los Lagos, Jalisco, Mexico

## Opening Prayer

O God, your divine energy fills North America with special places of great beauty and healing consolation. As I make a prayerful, imaginary pilgrimage to this holy ground, I bring to my prayer those in need and place them with me at these natural sources of your spirit. Hear these intentions for which I pray....

## Scripture Reading

Then Mary said, "Here I am, the servant of the Lord."

*Luke 1:38*

## Imagine

*Out here in the remote land beyond the mountains of central Mexico, in the year 1623, a mother prayed fervently before the image of the Virgin Mary, and her daughter, who seemed to be dead, was brought back to life.*

*That is why pious pilgrims of all ages, shapes and sizes still walk the fifty-five miles from San Miguel de Allende in central Mexico to the Basilica of Nuestra Señora de San Juan de los Lagos (Our Lady of Saint John of the Lakes) in the state of Jalisco. Join them as they trudge up the last mile toward the church on the hilltop.*

*At the crown of the hill, the circular dome of the church shines out of the haze. Two towers, slender and graceful, soar up like minarets and flank it. Their two crosses beckon the struggling pilgrims to climb just one more hill, as Jesus did to Calvary. You are in the midst of a colorful and motley group. Some tall men wear sombreros that bob and weave in the midst of shawl-covered women. Some carry banners; others, images of favorite saints; others, lunch buckets. One thing they all have in common—dust-covered and worn-looking boots and shoes.*

*You are at the top of the hill now, at the church door. The air is darkened with dust from the tromping feet. Enter the church now and be dazzled by the explosion of light! Everything in front of you is a kaleidoscope of gold, silver, white marble. Towering candlesticks perch on a marble altarpiece. The Virgin looks down from a high perch on the altarpiece, but her gaze is compassionate, understanding. She too once trudged through the desert. She understands the pain of those who mill below. Greet her: "Hail Mary, full of grace!" Rest a moment under her gaze.*

*Now go into the "chapel of miracles." There hang tokens of gratitude and petitions—a red number 18 soccer shirt, a framed picture of a handsome man, small photos, rosaries, knee braces, serapes, images of the virgin—each telling its own story of hope, of prayer, of pilgrimage, of graces received.*

*Here you can place your own burdens and pray for your own miracles.*

## CONCLUDING PRAYER

Saint John, who stayed with Mary, the mother of Jesus, at the foot of the cross, please intercede for my words of petition....

# Pilgrimage to
## the Old Faithful Geyser,
## Yellowstone National Park,
## Wyoming

## Opening Prayer

O God, your divine energy fills North America with special places of great beauty and healing consolation. As I make a prayerful, imaginary pilgrimage to this holy ground, I bring to my prayer those in need and place them with me at these natural sources of your spirit. Hear these intentions for which I pray....

## Scripture Reading

Jesus said, "Everyone who drinks this water will get thirsty again and again. Everyone who drinks the water I give will never thirst—not ever. The water I will give will be an artesian spring within, gushing fountains of endless life.

*John 4:13-14*

## Imagine

*Visit the Old Faithful Geyser in Yellowstone National Park in Wyoming in the wintertime, when all is stark and defined by three colors: the green of the forest, the black stumped residue of old fires, and the pristine white snow.*

*As you stand looking forward, two magnificent fir trees, one to the left and one to the right, margin your view. Framed in the center is a small dome with steam leaking forth as from a teapot.*

*Directly behind the dome is a hillock. Younger trees are a verdant green, but sprinkled between them are the blackened stumps of their forebears. They stand stark against the ermine snow.*

*Watch and wait. Be there with the gentle steam rising out of the "teapot" dome. It says, "Something's brewing! Just you wait. You will see." Be patient.*

*Suddenly, there is a hissing sound. And faithful as always, a geyser of steam begins to rise against the sky: higher, and higher, and higher; 180 feet today; 8400 gallons of water. Marvel at the white steam filigreeing the blue sky.*

*Be still, and know that God is God.*

## Concluding Prayer

O God, help me know that you are steadfast in your love, as I pray these petitions....

# Pilgrimage with the Swallows
## of San Juan Capistrano, California

## Opening Prayer

O God, your divine energy fills North America with special places of great beauty and healing consolation. As I make a prayerful, imaginary pilgrimage to this holy ground, I bring to my prayer those in need and place them with me at these natural sources of your spirit. Hear these intentions for which I pray....

## Scripture Reading

Joseph, chagrined but noble, determined to take care of things quietly so Mary would not be disgraced.

*Matthew 1:19*

## Imagine

*You are in the old Mission garden of San Juan Capistrano, California, for the annual celebration of the "Return of the Swallows." It is March 19, the Feast of St. Joseph.*

*Red bougainvilleas drape themselves over an archway. White water lilies float on the surface of an old Moorish fountain in the center of the patio. All is serene and calm. On every side you are encircled by verdant shrubbery. The dawn has just broken in the eastern sky. Slowly the bells begin to toll announcing the Feast Day and beckoning the birds.*

*You and other pilgrims gathered there look skyward. Soon black dots appear on the horizon. They loom larger and larger until they can be seen to dart and swoop. In the old courtyard, there is a hum of excitement among the waiting pilgrims, for they are glimpsing an odyssey that is older than these mission stones. No doubt the ancestors of these swallows visited Cap-istrano before any human ever arrived.*

*Soon the first swallows arrive and begin to claim their places in the mission garden. Their journey has been long and some-times heroic. They have winged their way north all the way from Goya in Argentina! If they could speak, what tales they could tell of such an epic journey. Instead, with full-throated joy they sing a song of homecoming. Hear their song! Hear the bells of the mission welcome them!*

## Concluding Prayer

Saint Joseph, lift my heart with the swallows' song, help me on the journeys I need to take in my life....

# Pilgrimage to the Shrine of Our Lady of the Snows, Belleville, Illinois

## Opening Prayer

O God, your divine energy fills North America with special places of great beauty and healing consolation. As I make a prayerful, imaginary pilgrimage to this holy ground, I bring to my prayer those in need and place them with me at these natural sources of your spirit. Hear these intentions for which I pray....

## Scripture Reading

You're so blessed among women,
and the babe in your womb, also blessed!

*Luke 1:40*

## Imagine

*The shrine of Our Lady of the Snows contains a variety of gardens, shrines, grottos, and a magnificent basilica. Our Lady of the Snows is one of the oldest of Marian devotions, going all the way back to a legend from the year 352 A.D. It is believed that Mary appeared then to a Roman couple and asked that a church be built.*

*The location? Mary indicated it should be built on a "place where snow would fall," and lo and behold, snow did fall in Rome on the almost impossible date of August 5. So a church was built on that location—the Esquiline Hill in Rome. Many churches have been built on that site over the centuries, including the most recent Basilica of Saint Mary Major.*

*For our pilgrimage to Belleville, Illinois, we will climb to the highest knoll on the shrine property. There we approach the Annunciation garden. Before us is a wall fronted by a reflecting pool. Mounted on the wall are two larger-than-life images—one of the Blessed Virgin Mary, the other of the Angel Gabriel proclaiming the Annunciation.*

*The area behind the images is filled with both deciduous and fir trees of different shades of green. In the reflecting pool, which is situated in front of the Annunciation scene, a lovely fountain gurgles and leaps up. Across the pool, four large bronze bells stand anchored by copper Byzantine turrets. Every hour these bells toll proclaiming the good news of salvation.*

*Stand before these images. Hear the bubbling water. Be soothed by the green surroundings. Listen to the bells tolling out the hour.*

## CONCLUDING PRAYER

Our Lady, Help of Christians, as you welcomed the message of the angel, please welcome my petitions...

# Pilgrimage to
# the World Trade Center,
# New York City

## Opening Prayer

O God, your divine energy fills North America with special
places of great beauty and healing consolation. As I make a
prayerful imaginary pilgrimage to this holy ground, I bring to my
prayer those in need, and place them with me at these natural
sources of your spirit. Hear these intentions for which I pray…

## Scripture Reading

And those eighteen in Jerusalem the other day, the ones crushed
and killed when the Tower of Siloam collapsed and fell on them,
do you think they were worse citizens than all other Jerusalem-
ites? Not at all.

*Luke 13:4*

## Imagine

*Go back some years to a time right after the twin towers of
the World Trade Center collapsed on 9/11. You are flying at
night into New York from Europe. Below is the inky blackness
of ocean, but on the horizon there is a great glow.*

*The pilot announces: "We're beginning our approach into New
York City, and we'll fly directly over the Statue of Liberty."
Soon enough, there she stands, her illumined torch thrusts toward the stars. What a magnificent sight! And just across, on
the shore, lighted skyscrapers ring Manhattan Island. Quickly
look to the right to see the Brooklyn Bridge sucking up the traffic and pouring it out of downtown.*

*But now the pilot says, "Look right below. See the black square surrounded by lights? That is Ground Zero, the wound left on the city when the twin towers fell."*

*Ponder all the hopes and dreams of so many innocents plunged into that dark hole of sadness in a single moment. This black patch is holy ground. This black patch is a badge of courage that reminds us of the innocent victims of terrorism and war throughout our world.*

## CONCLUDING PRAYER

Dear God, help me remember the innocent victims of war and terrorism on all sides....

# Pilgrimage to the White Dove of the Desert, Tucson, Arizona

## Opening Prayer

O God, your divine energy fills North America with special places of great beauty and healing consolation. As I make a prayerful, imaginary pilgrimage to this holy ground, I bring to my prayer those in need and place them with me at these natural sources of your spirit. Hear these intentions for which I pray....

## Scripture Reading

At once, the same Spirit pushed Jesus out into the wild. For forty wilderness days and nights he was tested by Satan.

*Mark 1:12-13*

## Imagine

*Today in the desert outside Tucson, the giant saguaro cacti lift their arms towards the sky as though in prayer. Just beyond the whirring traffic on Interstate 10, wild mustangs kick up a cloud of dust on the horizon. And the relentless desert sun pushes the temperature well above 100 degrees.*

*Looming up out of the sea of brown parched desert is an oasis, the "White Dove of the Desert," the Mission of Saint Francis Xavier. Its two classic Moorish towers are snow white and its ornamented façade a desert brown.*

*On April 28, 1700, Father Kino, S.J., the first missionary in the area, wrote in his diary that he was laying the foundations of a very large and spacious church and that all the people were working on it with much pleasure and zeal.*

*That was the dream, but later in that century the Jesuits were suppressed and the original mission abandoned. It would be left to the Franciscans in 1797 to build the present "Dove of the Desert" mission near Tucson, Arizona, although it remained dedicated to the great Jesuit missionary.*

*Imagine coming out of the desert heat into the cool interior of the church. Before you looms a great and intricately carved and gilded gold altarpiece. On the top niche is an icon of Our Lady, and one notch below is the image of St. Francis Xavier, clad in black Jesuit cassock and white stole. Reflect on the fidelity of all the people who have built and maintained this church so that you might visit here.*

## CONCLUDING PRAYER

Saint Francis Xavier and Father Kino, I need your help remaining faithful to....

# Pilgrimage to Wrigley Field, Chicago, Illinois

## Opening Prayer

O God, your divine energy fills North America with special places of great beauty and healing consolation. As I make a prayerful imaginary pilgrimage to this holy ground, I bring my prayer those in need, and place them with me at these natural sources of your spirit. Hear these intentions for which I pray…

## Scripture

Reach out your hand to the homeless, the needy,
and your blessing will be full.

*Proverbs 7:32*

## Imagine

*Diamonds can be a girl's best friend; they can also be a boy's. We're talking baseball diamonds here, where the drama of being "safe!" or "out!" can mirror in some ways the drama of our lives.*

*Nowhere in North America is there a more iconic baseball diamond than the one at Wrigley Field in Chicago. (OK, there is Fenway and Yankee Stadium as well, but Wrigley will do for today.)*

*It is a sunny June day, and you are making a pilgrimage to a beloved ballpark right in the heart of Chicago's north side. Walk along the concourse under the stands. Buy yourself a hot dog and smear it with mustard (no ketchup allowed in Chicago). Walk through the tunnel that opens up into a glorious sight: a diamond trimmed with real grass spread out before you, an outfield with no clutter of billboards and real ivy covering the brick walls. This park is as all parks should be: alive!*

*The first inning unfolds. The white-jerseyed Cubs, with their blue and red caps, have loaded the bases. Hear the expectant murmur of the crowd, the chant of the vendors. Suddenly, the crack of the bat. A single to left. The base runners take off. The man on third scores easily. The man on second rounds third, heading for home. There is going to be a play. The blur of the ball is zinging toward home plate. The runner slides. The catcher blocks the plate. There is a cloud of dust and you see the umpire's arms stretch out: "SAFE!"*

*The player is safe at home, as are we. Is that is not what all our hearts seek?*

CONCLUDING PRAYER:

Lord, there are many people wishing to be safe at home; let me remember these....

# PART IV

## LITANIES

*The praying of litanies is common in many cultures, places and religions. The rhythmic repetition of words, names and titles lends itself to spiritual remembrance and reflection. Here are two contemporary litanies that are uniquely North American. The first invokes North American saints and holy people; the second gives thanks for the varied and holy work of all workers.*

# A North American Litany of Saints

*This is a litany of North American saints and holy people. There may be saints not listed, and some here have not yet been canonized. Still, this litany demonstrates the number and diversity and strength of the holy people who have graced the North American continent. We will continue to add names to this litany. You may wish to personalize these intentions by adding particular intentions to individual saints that you feel appropriate to your own personal needs.*

**All you holy saints of Canada…pray for us.**

Saint Marguerite Bourgeoys (housekeeper and foundress of the Congregation of Notre Dame of Montreal): bless our daily work.

Saint Marie Marguerite D'Youville (wife, mother, widow, foundress of a community of "Grey Nuns"): bless our families and loved ones.

Saint René Goupil (lay medic and Jesuit martyr): give safe passage to those who travel today.

Blessed Brother André Bessette (doorkeeper and healer at St. Joseph Oratory in Montreal): bring healing hospitality to those in need.

Saint John de Lalande (layman and martyr): grant courage to the dispirited.

Blessed Maria Catherine of St. Augustine (Sister of Mercy, who died at age 36): help us grow in compassion.

**All you native-born saints of North America…pray for us.**

Blessed Kateri Tekakwitha ("Lily of the Mohawks" and patron of the environment): open our eyes to the truth.

Saint Katharine Drexel (philanthropist and foundress of the Sisters of the Blessed Sacrament): help us to be poor in spirit in the consumer culture.

Saint Elizabeth Ann Seton (wife, mother, widow, foundress
of the American Sisters of Charity): bless all who grieve
the loss of a loved one.

Saint Juan Diego (visionary of Our Lady and the miracle
of the roses): may roses of compassion bloom for all those
in the midst of estrangement.

Blessed Dina Belanger of Quebec (concert musician and
member of the Religious of Jesus and Mary): may soothing
music calm all troubled hearts,

Blessed Carlos "Charlie" Rodriguez of Puerto Rico (promoter
of lay ministry): help all laypeople give loving service
to church and world.

Venerable Pierre Toussaint (former slave in Haiti, hairdresser,
husband and adoptive father, philanthropist in New York
City): may we be generous with family, friends and
strangers alike.

**All you holy missionaries to the New World…pray for us.**

Pedro de Corpa (and the other slain friars of Georgia)
let us imitate your courage.

Juan de Padilla (missionary to the North American plains):
may we share your energy.

Blessed Junípero Serra (founder of the California Missions):
help us follow our own missionary paths in our daily lives.

Saint Rose Philippine Duchesne (missionary to Native
Americans along the Mississippi, who called her *Quah-
kah-ka-num-ad*—"Woman who prays always"): may we
pray for others always.

Saint Mother Theodore Guèrin (missionary and foundress
of the Sisters of Providence of Indiana, who dealt with
very difficult superiors): help us confront unjust authority
with strength and compassion.

Saint John Neumann (bishop, builder of churches and schools
in Philadelphia, Pennsylvania): bless all students and
their teachers.

Saint Frances Xavier Cabrini (missionary to Italian-American immigrants): give all those in need the care they deserve.

Blessed Francis Xavier Seelos (imaginative preacher who was the victim of jealousy): help us remain free from gossip, false judgment and envy.

Saint Isaac Jogues (and the other North American martyrs): may we too be courageous and faithful in the face of fear and violence.

**All you saints and martyrs of Mexico and Central America...pray for us.**

Saint Manuel Morales (Mexican martyr and twenty-eight-year-old husband and father of three): help us always care for the young.

Saint Anthony Mary Claret (writer and "Spiritual Father of Cuba," founder of the Claretians): bless all messengers of the Good News.

Saint Salvador Lara Puente (Mexican martyr and twenty-one-year-old mining worker): let our youth have the courage of their convictions.

Archbishop Oscar Romero (El Salvadoran bishop and martyr, killed at the altar while celebrating Mass): may we all thirst for justice and peace.

Blessed Ramon Vargas Gonzalez (Mexican martyr and medical student): bless all doctors, nurses and caregivers.

Maryknoll Sisters Maura Clark and Ita Ford, Ursuline Sister Dorothy Kazel, and lay missioner Jean Donovan (all murdered for working among the poor of El Salvador): may we imitate your courage and dedication.

Blessed José Sanchez del Rio (fourteen-year-old Mexican martyr): help us sustain and nourish our young people.

Blessed Luis Padilla Gomez (president of Mexico's Young Catholic Association): bless the youth who are struggling in their process of growth.

Sister of Notre Dame de Namur Dorothy Stang (the "Martyr of the Rainforest," killed in Brazil for defending the rights of peasants against loggers and ranchers): help us understand and take responsibility for the consequences of our actions.

Blessed Miguel Agustín Pro (and the twenty-five other martyrs of Mexico): help us honor Christ by helping to bring about his kingdom on earth as it is in heaven.

Saint Rafael Guizar Valencia (Mexican bishop and missionary who had a special interest in the education of priests): may every Christian accept his or her vocation in life.

Saint Rodrigo Aguilar Alemán (and five other Mexican priests and martyrs who were members of the Knights of Columbus): help us always stand up for what we believe.

# The Litany of Work

We give thanks, O God, for the work of our lives.
>  We praise you, God.

For the work of our hands, *We praise you, God.*
For the work of our minds, *We praise you, God.*
For the work of our hearts, *We praise you, God.*

**Response to all: *We praise you, God.***

For the enlightening work of teachers, librarians, students
>  and coaches,

For the healing work of doctors, nurses and counselors,
For the creative work of artists, musicians, painters and sculptors,
For the precise work of engineers, scientists and computer
>  specialists,

For the nurturing work of homemakers, parents and guardians,
For the wise work of retirees and grandparents,
For the proclaiming work of writers, photographers,
>  editors and publishers,

For the trustworthy work of accountants, bankers, lawyers,
>  politicians and salespeople,

For the faith-filled work of ordained, religious and lay ministers,
For the protective work of police, firefighters and military
>  personnel,

For the dedicated work of secretaries, receptionists and
>  bookkeepers,

For the compassionate work of volunteers,
For the judicious work of managers, administrators, directors
>  and supervisors,

For the fruitful work of farmers, fishers, growers and gardeners,
For the steadfast work of those who manufacture things,
For the constructive work of builders, surveyors, architects,
>  masons and carpenters,

For the efficient work of those who transport people and
    things by bus, train, plane, taxi, truck and boat,
For the clarifying work of television, radio and news media
    workers,
For the dependable work of telephone and postal workers,
For the good work of all other workers,

For our work that sheds light on the darkness,
    *We praise you, God.*
For our work that creates order from chaos,
    *We praise you, God.*
For our work that builds peace out of hostility,
    *We praise you, God.*
For our work that helps others,
    *We praise you, God.*
For our work that serves others,
    *We praise you, God.*
For our work that empowers others,
    *We praise you, God.*
For our work that inspires others,
    *We praise you, God.*
For our work that enriches and ennobles all creation,
    *We praise you, God.*

# Sources of Quotes

Excerpt from page 6 of *Black Elk Speaks: Being the Life Story of a Holy Man of the Oglala Sioux* by John G. Neihardt. Used by permission of the University of Nebraska Press. Copyright © 1932, 1959, 1972 by John G. Neihardt; © 1961 by the John G. Neihardt Trust; © 2000 by the University of Nebraska Press.

Excerpt from "The Litany of Mary of Nazareth" by Pax Christi USA, the national Catholic peace movement, www.paxchristiusa.org. Adapted from Pax Christi USA's "Litany of Mary of Nazareth" prayer card (by Jean Wolbert, OSB, in collaboration with Anne McCarthy, OSB, and Margaret Wehrer) and words spoken by John Paul II. Copyright 1987. Available in Spanish and English. Used with permission.

"The Litany of Work" by David and Angela Kauffman, copyright © 1992 ACTA Publications, 5559 W. Howard Street, Skokie, IL 60077. Used with permission. All rights reserved.

**The following were used with permission of the authors:**

"The Our Father" and "The Hail Mary" © 2007 by Gregory F. Augustine Pierce.

Adaptation of the prayer to Saint Vincent de Paul by Voice of the Poor. See their website at www.voiceofthepoor.org.

"Come Sophia" by Miriam Therese Winter, copyright © Medical Mission Sisters, 1995.

"Good Morning, Americas" by Maureen P. Kane. See her website pertaining to Buffalo, NY, at www.missingbuffaloblog.com.

"God Is Good" by David Franzblau. At the time of this publication, Franzblau is a student at Sophia Institute, Holy Names College, Oakland, CA.

Excerpt from "Spirituality and Contemporary Culture—II" by Joan Chittister. Copyright © 2000 National Forum of The Center for Progressive Christianity, Irvine, CA (June 1-3, 2000).

Excerpt from *Pueblo and Mission, Cultural Roots of the Southwest* copyright © 1997 by Susan Lamb Bean. Northland Publishing Co., P.O. Box 1389, Flagstaff, AZ 86002-1389.

Unpublished poem © 2007 by Joyce Rupp.

# Acknowledgments

For a lived example of prayerful pilgrimage that inspired me to write the pilgrimage journeys for this book, I thank Rich Vacek (1944-2006). On his pilgrimage through leukemia, he prayed: "I continue to ask Jesus to walk with me daily and to heal me. I also ask Mother Mary to embrace me in her arms every day and give me comfort."

Father Gary Ostrander led me to contemporary Scripture. Joyce Rupp continues to inspire and encourage me.

Maureen Kane and Alison Byland volunteered editing help, and Father Tom Ward advised me on the pilgrimages.

Marcia Broucek and Greg Pierce completed the edit. Pat Lynch made it sing with her design and typesetting. Tom Wright did a handsome job on the cover.

# About the Author

William John Fitzgerald—"Father Fitz"—is a retired priest of the Archdiocese of Omaha, Nebraska, now residing in Scottsdale, Arizona, at Our Lady of Perpetual Help parish, where he continues to write, present adult workshops, oppose war, work to reform the church, root for the Diamondbacks, and minister to the poor.

He has traveled to many of the sites in this book. Others he has seen in his imagination.

Three of his other books are available from ACTA Publications:

> *100 Cranes: Praying with the Chorus of Creation*
> *A Contemporary Celtic Prayer Book*
> *Diamond Presence: Twelve Stories of Finding God
>     at the Old Ball Park* (contributor)

His book *Seven Secrets of the Celtic Spirit* is available from Ave Maria Press.

You can visit the author at www.homestead.com/fatherfitz.

# Additional Books on Prayer and Spirituality

### A Contemporary Celtic Prayer Book
*by William John Fitzgerald*
*with a Foreword by Joyce Rupp*
Done with a Celtic sensibility, using ancient and contemporary prayers, this unique prayer book contains a simplified Liturgy of the Hours plus Celtic blessings, prayers and rituals for special occasions. 148-page paperback, $9.95

### Allegories of Heaven
### An Artist Explores the "Greatest Story Ever Told"
*by Dinah Roe Kendall*
with "The Message" text by Eugene H. Peterson
Contemporary English artist Dinah Roe Kendall offers a vibrant visual retelling of the full scope of Jesus' ministry through her figurative and narrative paintings, accompanied by Eugene Peterson's widely acclaimed contemporary rendering of the Bible. 100-page, four-color hardcover, $14.95

### Running into the Arms of God
### Stories of Prayer/Prayer as Story
*by Patrick Hannon*
Stories of prayer in everyday life tied to the traditional hours of the monastic day: matins, lauds, prime, terce, sext, none, vespers, compline. 128-page hardcover, $15.95; paperback $11.95

### Prayers from around the World and Across the Ages
*compiled by Victor M. Parachin*
A wealth of sublime, reverent and poignant prayers from many of the world's greatest spiritual practitioners, preceded by a one-paragraph biography of the person who composed it. 160-page paperback, $9.95

### Praying the New Testament as Psalms
*by Desmond O'Donnell and Maureen Mohen*
A unique new way to experience the riches of the New Testament through 100 original prayers, each arranged in a psalm-like format. 216-page paperback, $12.95

Available from booksellers or call 800-397-2282
www.actapublications.com